Taking up the challenge

by

Eric Hatton

Published by
Saturday Night Press Publications
Beaconsfield, England.

snppbooks@gmail.com

ISBN 978-0-9557050-7-6

Printed by
Lightning Source
www.lightningsource.com

Cover photographs by Magnus Smith

Music is in souls a sympathy with sounds;
And as the mind is pitched the ear is pleased
With melting airs, or martial, brisk or grave.
Some chord in unison with what we hear
Is touched within us – and the heart replies.

William Cowper

Dedication

I devote this book to Heather, my darling wife, who never failed in her love and support for me, and always showed me great affection. She sacrificed her own talents over our fifty years of marriage.

To my sister Laura for her love and inspired compositions of poetry and hymns, which matched my own views.

To my gentle, loving mother and father for so many things we invariably take for granted and only in retrospect see how much these have helped to mould us.

To my friend and colleague Gordon Higginson, whose demonstrations, conveying proof of the afterlife, brought consolation to me and countless others.

To Percy Brown and Derek Westlake, my business colleagues, who guided me into avenues of discovery through philosophical books and conversation.

To Harold Vigurs and Pop Jermy, Heather's dad, who in our long talks together opened my mind to the reality and immensity of the universe.

To Tom and Mabel Hibbs, whose Welsh house was my second home. They showed me the evidential realities of Spiritualism, how important it was to reveal truth, and introduced me to many who played a great part in my life.

My thanks and tributes can never be adequate for all my daughter Lisa and son Jonathan have done. They have cared for me and shown me tender love and patience, and by their example have encouraged their children to do the same.

How remiss it would be for me to fail to acknowledge the friendship and excellent mediumship of Sally Ferguson, Micky Wright (Ellis), Eileen Davies and Gerard Smith.

There are so many friends, too numerous to mention by name, who, each in their own way, have contributed to what I am.

Albert (Bert) Donald Hatton
who started it all
1924 - 1946

Contents

Foreword

As a young reporter working for a weekly Spiritualist newspaper, *Psychic News*, in the early 1960s, I had the wonderful opportunity of seeing some of the UK's top mediums demonstrate spirit communication at London's largest public venues. The evidence they provided, which formed the basis of my regular reports, was usually impressive and is there to view, in black and white, for anyone who has the time to search through the archives.

Though they made a huge impact on me at the time, I confess that without reading those reports to jog my memory, I would be hard pressed to recall even small details from the messages I heard.

But one memory has remained with me over those years. It was the solo performance of a debonair young man whose beautiful singing voice was matched by the passion and conviction with which the song or hymn was sung. That person was Eric Hatton, a Midlands businessman who has devoted most of his adult life to promoting Spiritualism's philosophy.

I was always delighted when I attended those big public demonstrations of mediumship to see Eric's name on the programme. It meant not only that we would be treated to a superb musical interlude but, when he was also the speaker, his words of wisdom on survival of death and the evidence that was available to those prepared to explore the subject.

That was something he had done, in his early days, and which he has actively encouraged others to do ever since.

By the time I got to know Eric and his lovely wife Heather they were both prominent Spiritualists, not only in the Midlands, and particularly at their local church in Stourbridge, but also at a national level. And when we have met it has usually been to discuss issues of the day, rather than reminisce about early days.

So, for me, one of the joys of the autobiography you are about to read is that, for the first time, Eric is sharing some of his early experiences with a wider audience, which helps us understand why he and Heather have devoted so much of their lives to Spiritualism.

Organisations of all shapes and sizes attract a variety of people into their fold and not all of them have the right motives. For some it can be a power trip: a way of cloaking themselves in an aura of authority as they clamber over others in the scramble to the top.

Eric Hatton certainly got to the top in Spiritualism, serving as president of the Spiritualists' National Union (SNU), which is widely regarded as the largest Spiritualist organisation in the world, and taking on many other responsibilities. But no one who knows Eric would believe he did so for any other reason than to serve those in the next world in their important mission of spreading the word about our continuing existence beyond death.

Indeed, it cannot have been easy for Eric and Heather to cope simultaneously with the demands of their business and those of national Spiritualism. But cope they did, even when those around them were in dispute. In that respect, Eric takes us behind the scenes to events that led to his resignation as SNU president. In doing so, with typical diplomacy and always a gentleman, he simply provides the facts – never before told – and leaves the reader to draw his or her own conclusions.

It is when he shares with us some of his personal mediumistic experiences that Eric's account takes on special significance. It was these paranormal events, after all, that formed the foundation on which his life of service has been based. And since he tells of the most amazing phenomena in such down-to-earth language, his testimony carries even greater weight.

Some of these happenings are so extraordinary – including witnessing several fully-formed materialised spirits walking and talking in good light – that many readers may doubt Eric's testimony, and even his sanity. But not those who know him. Careful, cautious and considered, he would be the perfect witness in a court of law.

It may surprise Eric to learn that his singing voice had as much impact on me as the mediums with whom he shared platforms. He will probably be just as surprised that there is any interest in his autobiography – after all, it's usually successful mediums who write books. But those who know a good story when they see one – as his editorial collaborator Susan Farrow certainly does – realise that Eric Hatton's life and work deserve to be shared with as wide an audience as possible. It's a story that is crying out to be told.

You are about to meet a very remarkable man who not only preaches Spiritualism but lives it.

Roy Stemman
November 2010

Editor's Introduction

I was first privileged to meet Eric Hatton when he visited me in my office at *Psychic News* in March 2008, just a few weeks after I had been appointed editor.

For some years I had known the name of this man who was held in such high esteem within the Spiritualist movement, and had read much about him. I was therefore keen to meet him in person. As we shook hands I realised in an instant what so many have realised before me – that Eric Hatton is unique.

After this first meeting I determined to do an extensive interview with Eric for *Psychic News*. On hearing my proposal he agreed with characteristic generosity and a few weeks later gave me a lengthy and frank interview covering a wide range of matters relating to Spiritualism.

Though this interview ran over two issues of the paper there was a large amount of material which was not included for reasons of space. In addition, during the course of the interview Eric and I had discussed many aspects of the movement, past and present, and found much common ground. There was more to be said – much more – and I began to ponder a means of drawing on his vast experience and knowledge for the benefit of a far wider readership.

By July 2008 I had a firm instinct that there should be a book about Eric's sixty-plus years at the heart of Spiritualism. But there was a problem. His inherent humility and modesty had always prevented him from consenting to the writing of such a book and I knew it would be an uphill struggle to persuade him of the importance of it.

By this time Eric had become a trusted friend and adviser, someone who, I knew, would always give me an honest opinion on the changes I was then planning at *Psychic News*. Time and again he provided me with wise guidance, sometimes gently preventing me from taking a rash or unwise step. For me, as for many others, he has been a patient listener, truthful even when it was not what I wanted to hear.

Tentatively, I began to raise the issue of his memoirs. He did not rule out the idea but was decidedly reticent. Towards the end of 2008, he gave in to my pestering and agreed to collaborate with me in writing his story. Since that time, interrupted by periods of severe ill health, Eric has worked with me whenever possible to share his unique experiences, principally in Spiritualism, but also concerning his family and business life, and in numerous other aspects.

The process of working with Eric to produce the book you are now about to read has been a privilege for me. My respect and affection for him are boundless and I can think of no better role model for the Spiritualist than he.

I record here my heartfelt thanks to Eric for allowing this book to become a reality and I respectfully dedicate my small part in it to him, to his late wife Heather, and to my own beloved partner in spirit, Majo Topolovac.

Susan Farrow
December 2010

Chapter 1

The start of it all

I was born in the spring of 1926, during a time of great hardship for people in industrial areas. For quite a number of years I lived in Brierley Hill, a town famous for its iron and steel works and its glass making. It was also home to a very large factory called Marsh and Baxter, which processed York hams, pork pies, sausages and similar products.

My mother had been born in the same area and for a number of years lived with my grandmother in a corner shop. This arrangement afforded both her and my father the opportunity not only of looking after my grandmother as she grew older, but also of having a roof over their heads when times were difficult.

I'm told – and I don't know how true it is, I think it was said in jest – that after I was born I was shown to my grandmother, and the next day she died of shock! Well, I'm not sure I believe it, but if it's so then it's a mark against me!

In my early years I was prone to a considerable amount of illness, and there were many occasions when I suffered from chest and throat problems. At one point I contracted pneumonia, an event which gave rise to an experience I've never quite forgotten. As I lay in my bed, feverish and poorly, I was suddenly aware of being on top of the wardrobe, looking down at myself on the bed. The memory has stayed with me, though at the time I didn't know what to make of it, and nor did my mother or father. I suppose I went along with the idea that I was in some sort of delirium and should be excused on the grounds that I would get better soon.

My mother and father were both hard-working people. My father was in the building trade and wasn't always in work for long periods. He also suffered with rheumatism for most of his life. He was a very kindly man and I never recall him hitting or slapping me, or indeed my brother and sister. He would reprimand us, certainly, and he had good reason to do so, but other than that he was a gentle man and my mother was a very gentle lady.

I use the word 'lady' because the area in which we lived could be said to have been a little bit rough. Most of the people who lived in the streets near to our own were hard-working and industrious, employed at one or other of the nearby factories. My parents had the ability to get on well with all sorts of people, and most of the local folk were beholden to my mother at one time or another. She was kindly disposed to help those who were in need of comfort or solace, and in many cases were unable to pay for the food they bought from the shop. She would say to them, 'O don't worry, I'll put it on the bill', or on the 'strap' as they called it. In fact, my mother never really put it on anything – she relied on her wonderful memory. My father would often say to her, 'Floss' – that's what he called her, although her name was Florrie – 'you're a fool. Those people will never pay you.' And she would reply, 'Don't worry, they'll pay me one day. The good Lord will thank me for being able to help them.' Such was my mother's disposition.

I'm not sure that I can pinpoint any particularly startling occasion which caused me to attribute an event to my psychic ability or awareness. I do remember, however, that my father, who would sometimes go away for several days at a stretch to work in different parts of the country, and from time to time in Ireland, would say to me, 'While I'm away, make sure you feed the chickens.' He reared chickens because, of course, they were always something for the pot when the need arose, and taking care of them was one of the jobs I had to do in his absence.

Well, devil-like in the way of most young boys, I was chasing the chickens around one day and one of them broke its leg. I'm not quite sure how it happened, but it was a compound fracture and the bone stuck out of the poor little chicken's leg at an alarming angle. Needless to say, I was horrified, and very fearful that I would be pulled over the coals by my dad. Something had to be done. So, unbeknown to my mother, I went into the shop, and since we sold almost everything it was possible to sell, took some bandages and Vaseline from the shelves and hurried back to bind up the chicken's leg. I did my best but I was still very afraid it would not recover and I would be in for trouble. To my amazement, within a couple of days the chicken was running around the yard as though nothing had happened. I suppose I must have concentrated on healing it, and sure enough it continued to thrive. Looking back, it was perhaps the first indication that I might have some healing ability. Regrettably, this early success was to prove short lived. When the chicken was big enough it was cooked by my mother and served up as a delicious meal!

In summer, my sister Laura and I would turn our hands to a job that most children would love – we made ice cream and sold it. It was a lengthy process and quite labour intensive, involving an outer wooden drum linked to a metal contraption which enabled the apparatus to turn by means of a handle. A metal drum was placed inside the centre and filled with the custard or ice cream mixture we had made the night before. Ice was packed and sealed in the area between the wooden and metal drums and the whole would be clamped down. Then we would start to turn the entire thing with the handle, a process which seemed to go on for ages but was well worth the effort when the lovely soft ice cream emerged at the end. On hot summer days people would queue outside the shop and buy it for one old penny.

Near to the shop there was a man who sold and delivered bags of coal to houses in the neighbourhood. Bill Whitcombe was a small man and I marvelled at how he managed to heft those heavy bags of coal from his cart without apparent effort.

By contrast, his wife was a fairly well-built woman and perhaps laid down the law to poor old Bill a little too much. As a result he could often be seen imbibing a few beers too many!

At the end of a working day, the horse which had faithfully pulled his cart would be taken to a nearby field for a well-earned rest, and I would often ride it bare-back for the short journey. On one particular occasion, Bill released the horse from its bridle, and instead of slowing down and waiting for me to dismount as it usually did, the creature reared up and I was unceremoniously tossed to the ground, breaking my left arm in the process.

On another memorable occasion, unbeknown to my mother, I accompanied Bill in his horse trap on a journey which terminated at a pub several miles from home. It being a Sunday, he enjoyed a few extra pints and, as we made our way back towards home, fell sound asleep, leaving me to take the reins and drive the horse. I had not the slightest idea where we were, and how we got back home I shall never know, but the horse obviously knew its way from long experience.

When eventually we arrived, my mother was understandably most upset, since I was only nine years old at the time and she had had absolutely no idea where I was. Bill's wife took him seriously to task for his behaviour, not least because she had been slaving over a hot stove to produce the Sunday joint of roast beef, which was completely ruined by his late return!

* * * *

When I was about eleven years old I was taken ill with rheumatic fever and confined to bed for a considerable time. In those days rheumatic fever was a serious and unpleasant complaint and in consequence I wasn't allowed to do any exercise, or indeed anything at all that might put a strain on my heart. As a result of these restrictions I was unable to take the examinations which would have enabled me to go from

Florrie and Albert Hatton – my mother and father

With my mother and father in their latter years

the local school to the grammar school in Stourbridge, some three miles away. Thus a large part of my education was simply overlooked.

As the years went by, my sister Laura and brother Bert – both of whom had received a much better education than I – were always keen to help me, as also were my father and mother. Perhaps because of the interruptions to my schooling I never took much to reading at that time. Yet, as I will explain later, during my teens I began to read avidly, absorbing a great deal of material.

In those days people would leave school at fourteen and I had little choice but to take a job in a local factory. It wasn't a factory I liked; in fact, as I think back over the years, I hated it. It was a dangerous job they'd given me, sometimes requiring me to work under drop-forging hammers which were large and very heavy, and often propped up merely by pieces of wood. I was expected to work on dies which shaped the moulds out of which steel components were formed.

It was around this time that I was asked if I would like to volunteer for the Air Raid Precautions service (ARP), since help was badly needed. Although I had no real idea what I would be letting myself in for, I agreed.

Looking back, I think I must have been pretty green, for the working conditions were certainly less than luxurious. When on duty I was based in a small brick and concrete building lacking any home comforts, and boasting nothing more than plain walls, wooden benches, a small low-wattage electric light and a simple paraffin stove to keep us warm.

The rota required me to report to the post in the evening and stay until I was no longer needed. It was my job to act as a messenger, running from one post to another carrying messages as required, particularly when air raids were taking place. Wherever I went, my gas mask came with me, but fortunately I never had cause to use it.

Although the German bomber planes would fly over several times each night, their primary targets were the cities of Birmingham and Coventry, whereas I was based in

Brierley Hill. However, very early one morning, I was running from one post to another when, alarmingly close to me, a British Halifax bomber plane came tumbling out of the sky and crashed to earth. There was a deafening explosion and the ground beneath my feet seemed to shake. I rushed to see if I could do anything to help, but alas there were no survivors.

When a while later I joined my mother, father and sister Laura in our Anderson shelter, they were greatly relieved to see me, for they had been very concerned. Listening to my account of the night's events they begged me not to do any further ARP duty. Indeed, my father was even more emphatic and virtually forbade me to volunteer any more from that point.

Although I was tired at the end of the next working day, having lost so much sleep the night before, I have to confess that I did slip quietly out of the Anderson shelter when I was sure the others were asleep. George Burkes, the senior warden, was so pleased to see me that he presented me with half a bar of precious ration chocolate!

Three nights later, the sky was alive with bombers flying towards Birmingham. Anti-aircraft guns were firing noisily as our search lights swept across the sky, trying to pick out the German planes in their beams. I must admit I was more than a little nervous when a huge bomb exploded about 250 yards in front of me and hit the ground. The earth seemed to shake with the force of the impact. Nonetheless, my curiosity got the better of me and I went to see what was happening. I was met with a dreadful sight. What just a few moments earlier had been family homes were now engulfed in flames after being blown apart by the bomb.

When at last I arrived home, my parents were exceedingly upset, and though by then I was fifteen years old, grown up and earning my own living, I had little choice but to listen to their reprimand and offer them a solemn promise that I would give up being an ARP messenger once and for all.

While working for the ARP, I had decided to join the Air Training Corps as a preliminary to joining the Royal Air Force. I don't know how it came about, but after a little while

I was tested, along with my friends and colleagues, by the officers, and for some unfathomable reason was made a sergeant. My brother, two years older than I, was then under my leadership, as were many other fellows who were my seniors in age. I suppose they weren't very happy about it in the early days, but as time went by I think I became reasonably proficient at running the flight, under the supervision of a Flight Sergeant friend of mine and a Warrant Officer who soon became a friend.

My appetite for knowledge was strong, perhaps because of the many opportunities I had been forced to miss during my school years. Almost every night I would go to classes at the Air Training Corps and absorb as much information as I possibly could. I suppose I must have done fairly well, because one of the teachers who, by coincidence, had worked at the school I'd attended, took a particular interest in me. He and his wife were nice people and he encouraged me to visit their home, where he taught me the rudiments of mathematics and helped to educate me in many other ways.

As time went by I was promoted to Flight Sergeant when the friend who had held that position went into the Royal Air Force. My responsibilities were that much greater, of course, because we had about fifty young men in the flight at that time. A few officers of the squadron were involved in politics and one of them in particular took a liking to me. I've since been told that he wasn't always the favourite of those who knew him in everyday business affairs, but I can only speak as I find. Although I didn't see it at the time, he and another officer did much to help mould me, both in character and in relative fluency of thought and speech.

Over the previous few years I had become interested in various forms of the Christian religion. I had explored two Methodist churches, looked at the Christadelphians, attended the Salvation Army and briefly rubbed shoulders with the Plymouth Brethren. These last, I felt, were not overly keen on me and I broke away from them, which I suppose was my saving grace.

In my later teens I became very attached to the Anglican church in Brierley Hill and also to one in Hartshill, which was a mission church. I don't know how it happened, but something must have alerted me to the fact that there were other avenues to explore, avenues which extended beyond the rigid repetitions that took place Sunday by Sunday.

By the time I reached the last years of my teens, my brother had been in the Royal Air Force for some while. For my own part I had moved from one factory to another having tried but failed to get into the Air Force. They would not accept me because the factory in which I was working at the time was making valuable and important munitions and as a result it was decided that I must remain in my position there.

When my brother would come home on leave from places such as Enniskillen in Ireland, Tenby in South Wales and Ayr in Scotland, he would speak about the experiences he'd had in some of the Catalina flying boats, which took off on water, and also in the Sunderland flying boats, which were very large planes. On one occasion he brought with him a New Zealand-born colleague named Dusty Miller and they spent a few days' leave at home with us. Most evenings they would go out and enjoy themselves over a few glasses of beer – indeed I think that sometimes it was probably more than a few!

I'm not sure how the subject came up, but when they returned home one night my brother related a strange tale. He told us that in some of the flying boats in which he worked, both he and other crew members had 'seen' colleagues who had been killed in aircraft accidents. In essence it seemed that although these fellows were dead, they were actually walking along the gangway of the plane. Stranger still was the fact that one or other of these dead fellows would walk straight through my brother and Dusty Miller, and through various other crew members too, so my brother and his friend were not alone in having the experience.

As I've already said, I was somewhat steeped in the orthodox churches by then, so when I poured scorn on what they were saying, they challenged me that if I didn't believe them I should do some research and find out if what they were saying was true.

Meanwhile, my sister Laura, who was very bright, had taken an office job in Birmingham and was sometimes required to visit factories in the course of her work. On one such occasion she met a young man who, along with his parents, attended a Spiritualist church in Smethwick, on the outskirts of Birmingham. As a result of her conversations with him she became interested in, and almost convinced by some of the things she had heard. So it was that she joined in with Bert and Dusty, saying to me, 'Well, you challenge it, and find out whether it's really true that people who die continue to live in another dimension.'

Taking up their challenge, I began by attending a Spiritualist centre in a place called Lye, about two-and-a-half miles from where we lived. At first I was interested in the medium, a Mr Shanks, but after a while I became somewhat disillusioned. I believe his livelihood was provided by a gentleman who owned a large factory in the Birmingham area and enabled Mr Shanks to carry out his work as a medium. Because I wasn't too happy with the way things were conducted – though I can't say they were fraudulent or anything of that kind – I decided to sample the Spiritualist church in Union Street, Stourbridge, which still stands on the same site today.

In 1945 I went into the Royal Air Force, and because by then I was partially convinced about Spiritualism, on those occasions when I had to stay in camp over the weekend I would seek out a Spiritualist church in the area. Sometimes it would be several miles away and I would have to walk there and back because forces transport at the end of the war was in very short supply.

Over a period of time I watched and came to respect a number of mediums who gave demonstrations which were of great interest to me, and in consequence of this I became more and more convinced of the reality of an afterlife.

My brother Bert, who had by then been stationed at a number of locations around the world – the Middle East, Dar es Salaam, Ceylon, India – ended up at the Kai Tak base in Hong Kong. I still have a few of the letters he sent, in which he painted a vivid and fascinating picture of his experiences.

By 1946 he was working as a Flight Engineer on one of the vast Sunderland flying boats and was about to embark on his last flight before being demobbed and sent home. They were to take off at night from Singapore. Unfortunately, as the plane took off, things went badly wrong and it crashed into the water. We received a telegram from the Air Ministry informing us that Warrant Officer A.D. Hatton was missing, presumed killed. My parents, no less than my sister Laura and I, were absolutely devastated. There we were, looking forward so much to having him home with us in just a few days, but it wasn't to be.

We tried to ascertain from the Air Ministry exactly what had happened. Was Bert still alive? we wondered, reasoning that although he was missing, his plane had perhaps come down in the Malayan jungle or in some other remote location. We waited anxiously for news. A few weeks later we received confirmation from the Air Ministry that Bert was indeed dead. What they didn't tell us, however, and we only found out later through mediumship, was that he had been buried the very next day after he had been killed in the plane crash.

Time went by, and a young medium named Gordon Higginson, who had recently come out of the army, visited the church at Stourbridge. Laura and I went along to listen to him and found the place packed to capacity. To say the least, his evidence was remarkable. Weeks passed and we continued with our lives as best we could, though with many unanswered questions concerning my brother's death. Then, out of the blue, a letter dropped onto the door mat. Gordon lived in the town of Longton, near Stoke-on-Trent, and the letter had come from the secretary of Longton church, Billy Harratt. He wrote with the extraordinary news that my brother had manifested during one of Gordon's circles, at which a

Above left: Gordon Higginson, the young medium through whom Bert Hatton first manifested

Above right: Bert Hatton who lost his life when the Sunderland flying boat, on which he was the Flight Engineer, crashed into the sea

Below: A Sunderland flying boat

number of people had been present. Not only did he give my brother's full name – Albert Donald Hatton – he also gave the nickname that only my sister and I had ever called him – 'Kim'. In addition to all this we were given his full service number. As most of us know, the chances of correctly guessing all six lottery numbers are slight in the extreme, yet here, remarkably, was my brother's seven digit number, relayed to us in its precise order. We were also given information about the circumstances of his death, the way in which his plane had crashed into the sea and the fact that he had not survived but other crew members had – details that had not been offered to us by the Air Ministry.

As a result of this information we decided to make further enquiries and were eventually able to write to the officer who had piloted the plane. He replied, telling us about the crash and explaining that the reason Bert had not survived was because, as Flight Engineer, he had been in a part of the plane from which it was nigh on impossible to escape.

Bert's death was a great tragedy in our lives, yet Gordon Higginson had given us enormous comfort through his remarkable evidence. For me it put the cream on the cake, and from that point on I became absolutely convinced of the continuity of life.

Chapter 2

New beginnings

Double trouble in the RAF ✦ *Spiritual healing with Harry Edwards* ✦
Gathering evidence ✦ *A meeting that would change my life*

Although we had received marvellous evidence of Bert's survival, it could not take away the pain of our physical loss, and my parents, Laura and I were still distraught.

On occasions when Laura and I would travel by bus from our home to Stourbridge church, our mother sometimes accompanied us. While there, we met up with various people, and I well remember that one lady and her husband were especially good to us. The lady's name was Mary Wright, though she was known to her friends as Micky. After the service, she and her husband Eric would often take us home in their car – a kindness we greatly appreciated. As time went by we became very friendly, and that friendship blossomed into something of great and lasting respect.

Eventually, Laura decided to attend the church's awareness circle. It being a new experience for her, she sat quietly, taking in the atmosphere but saying little. After a while, a mediumistic lady named Hilda Perry asked if anyone knew a Bert. Minutes passed and no one claimed the name. Tentatively, Laura spoke up and said that she knew a Bert, whereupon Hilda said, 'He tells me he is your brother.' She then went on to give a detailed description of Bert's bedroom and possessions, adding, 'He is telling me that in a chest under the window he left a flying jacket.' This was correct.

She then told Laura that before she left home that evening she had picked up a photograph of Bert and kissed it. Bert had been there with Laura as she did so – just the two of them together. Laura confirmed that this was exactly what she had done. Finishing the message, Hilda said, 'He asks me to assure you that he is not far away and is frequently with you all.'

Despite this and many other comforting messages from Bert, and my absolute conviction that life was eternal, I still missed him greatly and would often become very upset. I vividly recall that on occasions when I was stationed in Yatesby and Manby I would sometimes be so full of sadness that I would go out in the evenings to the fields nearby the station and sit under the trees crying and crying, asking God why he had taken Bert away. I blamed God very considerably for what had happened and wondered constantly why it had to be.

As I continued to serve in the Royal Air Force, I enjoyed the welcome weekend diversion of playing football for Bath City and Grantham Town. It was a pleasant change from the routine of service life and I dare say the physical exercise and concentration required for it did much to distract me from the ever-present sadness of Bert's death.

Back at the station, I was singled out for something which in those days was a decidedly unusual trait: I was a vegetarian. I had made the decision to give up eating meat as a result of an earlier chance encounter with a man I had never previously met.

One night I had set off to walk the thirteen miles back from the outskirts of Bath after attending an awareness circle at the Spiritualist church in Manvers Place. I was hoping to be able to hitch a lift and was delighted when a car pulled up alongside me. As I climbed gratefully into the car, the driver introduced himself as Ivor Sercombe and asked what I had been doing in Bath. I debated for a moment what I should reply, and decided to say that I had been to a meeting.

'What kind of meeting?' he asked.

Resolving to be straightforward, I told him, 'I've been to a Spiritualist church.'

'That's very interesting,' he replied. 'I'm a medium.'

For the rest of the journey we talked about our common interest, and I found myself greatly impressed with both his knowledge and personality. I suppose he must also have been impressed by me because, before our shared journey was over, he had invited me for a meal with his wife and daughter at their home in Devizes.

He collected me on the appointed day and I quickly found out that Ivor and his family were strict vegetarians. During this and two subsequent visits we spoke at length about many things, including vegetarianism.

My early experiences of living near the Marsh and Baxter factory in Brierley Hill had alerted me to the fact that 100 pigs were brought there every day for slaughter, and I was concerned about the cruelty involved. My conversations with Ivor and his family awakened my desire to give up eating meat and I decided from that point on that I would become a vegetarian.

Meat-based meals were the norm amongst my RAF colleagues, and having no desire to make an issue of my preference for a meat-free diet, I dealt with the situation by making discreet trips to the rear of the food-serving counters at meal times in order to procure a piece of cheese and some salad or vegetables to accompany it. In due course it became apparent that this habit had been noted by the catering officer, and I was eventually summoned to his presence and asked to explain my 'strange' dietary requirements.

'What's this I hear about you wanting to be a vegetarian?' he asked.

'I am one,' I replied.

He then asked me if I was getting a balanced diet, to which I replied that I was not. On hearing this, he gave me permission to go and purchase some proper vegetarian food, telling me that on presentation of a bill I would be reimbursed.

All went well for several weeks, until news of my unusual diet reached the ears of the officer in charge of the station. The catering officer was ordered to present me to his office.

Air Commodore Spreckley sat stiffly behind his desk as I was marched in by the catering officer. He then proceeded to question me about why I wished to be a vegetarian, since it would cause trouble, he said.

I suppose he must have been displeased with my rather tremulous answers, for he instructed the catering officer that he should no longer pay me for food purchases, and instead should order and obtain the necessary vegetarian food supplies direct from the manufacturers.

The nerve-wracking interview apparently at an end, the catering officer was ordered to take me away. As I was marched towards the door, the Air Commodore barked, 'Wait! Have you got any other crackpot notions? For instance, what is your religion?'

'I am a Spiritualist, sir,' I replied.

'A what?' he demanded.

'A Spiritualist,' I repeated.

'Get him out!' he bawled at the catering officer. 'Get him out!'

There was no doubt about it – I was a marked man. Not only the first officially recorded vegetarian in the RAF, but a Spiritualist to boot!

In the way of those who were used to buying in bulk for the forces, the catering officer set about ordering a veritable mountain of food for me, but, in one of life's strange ironies, just a week or two later I was transferred from that station to another. I can only hope they found a good use for the large quantity of vegetarian food they had acquired!

* * * *

While at RAF Manby, near Louth, I would sometimes go to a small Spiritualist church in the town, where they seemed pleased to have an air force chap amongst them. On occasions when I had more spare time I would visit other churches and centres within a twenty-five-mile radius of the station. On some of these visits I would receive evidential spirit contacts; at other times, things were not so good.

The year 1947 was difficult. During that time I spent almost nine months under the care of one RAF hospital or another. Eventually it was decided that I should undergo spinal surgery in the hope of curing a problem which had troubled me over a long period and was causing me great pain. Because of the nature of the operation – a laminectomy – I was forced to lie on my stomach for several days while the wound began to heal.

During this rather depressing period I received an unexpected but most welcome visit, for which I am grateful to this day. My visitor was a Spiritualist minister named Albert Taylor, a man I had never previously met. Albert was very dedicated and had apparently heard on the Spiritualist grapevine that I had had an operation and was slowly recovering in hospital. He lived in Birmingham and the RAF hospital was in Cosford, several miles west of Wolverhampton on the Shropshire side. How on earth he made his way there I shall never know, for he didn't have a car and public transport was very poor at that time. I have never forgotten his kindness in making the

Albert Taylor

effort to see someone whom he felt it was his duty to visit, and in cheering me up, which he certainly did.

When I had recovered sufficiently to travel, I was instructed to return to my station at Manby in Lincolnshire. A few weeks later, the back trouble for which I had been treated began to manifest again and I had no choice but to return to the medical officers. After consultations with two of them I was sent down to a convalescent home at Newton Ferrers, in Devon. Having been given a warrant to travel, I decided to take a risk and stop off in London.

Harry Edwards, whose healing sanctuary was based at Burrows Lea in Surrey, a few miles outside London, was by this time a well-known and respected healer and, having had enough of the back problems which were causing me so much trouble, I had made up my mind to telephone him for an appointment.

Harry himself answered the phone when I called, and I asked if he could see me the next morning. He told me he was sorry but they did not do healing on that particular day. My heart sank at this and I told him that unfortunately it meant I wouldn't be able to come at all. When he asked why not, I said that I was in the RAF and was travelling from A to B. Immediately he said, 'Lad, I'll see you.' So I went down to his sanctuary and had healing from him. It was just Harry and me – there was no one else in sight.

Harry Edwards

So successful was the healing that when I got to the convalescent home a couple of days later and had a medical examination, the medics accused me of swinging the lead. I was sent straight back to duty and when finally I left the RAF in 1948 I was classed as 'A1'! What they didn't know was that I had been to see Harry Edwards, and that whatever was wrong with me, he had put right. Though I would come to know him very well in later life, that was my first great tribute to Harry and his excellent healing.

* * * *

Back in civilian life I began to work as a salesman, representing a company in Dudley which supplied greeting cards and related products. The job was challenging, requiring me to be on the road for much of the time, but I found it satisfying and infinitely preferable to the factory jobs I had held before joining the RAF. Since I was sometimes away overnight, I took the opportunity to visit mediums who did not have the slightest idea who I was. A number of these conveyed good evidence to me from my brother and other family members, as also did Sally Ferguson and Arthur Whyman at Stourbridge church, of which I had recently become a member.

I suppose my employer must have been persuaded that I was doing my work with some degree of competence because, to my surprise, after a year he promoted me to the rather grand-sounding role of sales manager when I was just twenty-four years old.

By this time, Laura and I had become quite friendly with a number of mediums, perhaps the most exceptional being Gordon Higginson and the Yorkshire-born Walter Brooks, who would sometimes visit our home. On one such occasion, as Gordon sat chatting with Laura, myself and our parents, he told us that there was a man from spirit wishing to make his presence felt.

'His name is Frank Hill,' Gordon said. 'He says he lived at number forty-four and passed with chest trouble. He is sending his love to his wife, Eliza Harriet.'

This surprised us, since although the other details were correct, Frank's wife was called Lila. We disputed the name but Gordon stuck to his guns. It was a mystery.

The next day she visited our shop and handed my mother her ration book so that some coupons could be removed. Mother took the opportunity to glance at the front cover, which bore the name E.H. Hill.

Intrigued, Mother asked what the E.H. stood for, but Mrs Hill refused to tell her, maintaining that she had always hated her name. After a lot of persuasion, she finally gave in and told Mother that her name was Eliza Harriet. 'Nobody's ever used it except my Frank,' she said, 'and he's dead now.'

On another occasion Gordon was sitting in our living room when he suddenly become aware of a lady in spirit who identified herself as Mrs Bullock. This lady communicated to him that she had lived next door to us prior to her passing some years earlier.

Her first name was Marie, Gordon told us, and her husband, who was still alive, was named George Henry. He added that the couple had three daughters, Mary, Gladys and Marian. We hadn't known that George Bullock's second name was Henry, but he confirmed it the next day when my dad asked him.

Mrs Bullock also conveyed to Gordon that when she had been on earth she would often fetch a jug of beer for her husband from the local pub and would have a quick swig from it herself before she delivered it to him!

Continuing with her evidence, Mrs Bullock told Gordon of her other next-door neighbour, mentioning that her name was Agnes Fowler but that everyone called her Aggie. This was true. He then surprised us by saying there were to be two future events relating to Aggie that would shock us.

A few days later Aggie came into our shop and told us that her mother had suffered a stroke. There was not much hope of recovery, she said. The lady died a few days later.

Some time afterwards, Marian Bullock came into the shop in some distress and asked my mother if she would accompany her to Aggie's house because she had found her lying on the floor and did not know what to do. It turned out that Aggie had also suffered a stroke and she died shortly afterwards. These unfortunate events were the two shocks which Mrs Bullock had successfully conveyed to Gordon from her side of life.

Walter Brooks provided us with some wonderful evidence over the years, but one of the most amusing examples occurred when he was staying with our parents, Laura and myself. As he relaxed one evening, chatting to my father, Walter said he was aware of a spirit lady who was also called Laura. He proceeded to give us a great deal of evidence from her about the childhood she had shared with my father – for she was his sister. So accurate was this evidence that my father, who rarely showed emotion, was in tears of joy. Walter went on to tell us that my Aunt Laura was laughing and saying something about drawers.

Walter Brooks

When she had passed on a few months before, she had left all her worldly goods to my father. There were not many items but they had been precious to her and my uncle. Dad thought Laura might have left a little money, but as we cleared her house we did not find any, and therefore believed she was now telling us to look for it in the drawers.

At Dad's request I had already taken various pieces of furniture to the warehouse in Cradley Heath and so we thought something must be concealed in a drawer of one of those pieces. I got out the car and Walter and I drove to

Cradley Heath in a state of high excitement. On arrival at the warehouse we set about an enthusiastic search of the furniture. Pulling out each of the drawers we could see nothing until we reached the very last one, at the back of which was a brown paper parcel. Oh, the excitement! We didn't open it there and then but took it back to Dad, since it belonged to him.

Delivering the precious parcel into his hands we watched intently as he unwrapped it, wondering just how much money was inside. Imagine our shock and surprise when we found that it contained three pairs of brand new ladies knickers!

When we had got over the disappointment, my sister said to our mother, 'I only spoke to you last night saying that I'd have to go and buy some new knickers!' Mother confirmed this. Walter had not been in our house when they had that conversation.

* * * *

In the early 1950s I drove Gordon Higginson to South Wales, where he was to demonstrate at a number of public meetings. We stayed with Tom and Mabel Hibbs, whose house had by this time become almost a second home to me. Alec and Daisy Leary were also there, since Alec would be the speaker at Gordon's meetings.

At the conclusion of the first meeting, held in Tonypandy, we all returned to the Hibbs' home, where Mabel's sister Abby had prepared freshly cooked ham accompanied by chips the like of which I've rarely tasted. We ate at a huge rectangular table, seven feet long and made of solid oak. There were nine of us for the meal, including Gordon Hibbs, Tom and Mabel's son.

After the excellent supper, we were chatting away when our conversation turned to the phenomenon of table movement. More in jest than with serious thought we wondered whether anything could be achieved with the very heavy table at which we were sitting. We cleared it completely and placed a séance trumpet in the middle of it. All the lights were extinguished, but a fire burning merrily in the hearth cast a glow throughout the room. We sang cheerful songs and Welsh hymns, never really thinking anything would happen, just being happy. Each of us placed both hands on the table and were amazed when after a short while we heard a tapping sound from inside the trumpet, which then started slowly to move around. Before long the motion became more rapid as the trumpet moved from person to person.

Someone suggested we should listen in case the trumpet had anything to tell us. Our hands were still on the table, clearly visible in the firelight, and to our great surprise we heard sounds coming from under the table, followed by sounds on its surface. We then felt a gentle movement of the table which after a moment or two became more pronounced, as did the psychic energy we were all feeling. Without further warning the table began to rise, our hands still upon it. We were stunned, and decided to take them off to see what would happen. The table continued to rise until it was several inches off the ground, after which it suddenly descended to the floor and everything was still. We were very excited, especially since none of us had been in trance and we had all witnessed what had taken place.

By this time it was about 2.30 in the morning and we all went to bed, some of us far too excited to sleep. The next morning Alec Leary, a scientist, went downstairs ahead of everyone, measured the table, and estimated that it weighed 200 lbs (90.5 kilos).

The next evening's public meeting took place in Cardiff, chaired by Mr Trenchard, a senior official at the docks. Afterwards, he offered us refreshments, but we politely declined them since we were desperate to experiment again with the table. We planned to replicate the exact physical conditions that had existed prior to the previous night's dramatic events. The fire burned in the grate, Abby cooked us the same meal, we all sat in the same places and sang the same songs. What happened? Precisely nothing!

As time went on, my conviction that life was eternal remained strong. I continued to research the subject of Spiritualism, reading books not only about the history of the movement, but also on a wide range of philosophical and spiritual matters. In the course of these researches I took the opportunity to watch yet more mediums at work and gained additional persuasive survival evidence in the process.

* * * *

Though I did not know it at the time, a higher power had taken a hand and would shortly lead me to a first meeting with the lady who would eventually become my wife.

Just five days before my own birth in 1926, Heather Jermy had been born on 5th March into a Spiritualist family in Ventnor on the Isle of Wight. Her childhood was a loving and happy one, shared with her older brother Dennis.

During the 1920s, Heather's father, Willie Jermy, had been a driving force in establishing Spiritualism on the island, and by 1938 his hard work came to fruition with the founding of a Spiritualist church in Victoria Street, Ventnor – the very first on the Isle of Wight. The church was dedicated by Ernest

Ventnor Spiritualist Church

Oaten, then editor of *Two Worlds*, and continues to flourish on the same site today.

Under Willie's leadership the church grew and thrived, attracting some of the finest mediums and speakers of the day. It was not uncommon for luminaries of the Spiritualist movement such as Hannen Swaffer, Helen Hughes, Nan McKenzie, Harry Edwards, Bertha Harris and Ernest Oaten to take to the platform in Ventnor, many of them staying with Willie and his wife Lily.

So it was that Heather grew up immersed in a world where the Spiritualist ethos was an accepted and fundamental part of life. For her, belief in the spirit world was as natural as breathing; indeed, she was endowed with a mediumistic gift herself.

Heather encountered many fine mediums during her childhood, and perhaps the most remarkable of her experiences came with the visit of the famous materialisation medium Helen Duncan. Mrs Duncan was staying as a guest in the Jermy home and had agreed to give a materialisation séance for a number of invited sitters.

Although Heather was entirely at ease with mediumship, she was only about nine years old at the time of Mrs Duncan's visit and thus was told that she could not attend the séance and must go to bed. Being inquisitive, she didn't like this one bit and decided to creep quietly down the stairs with the intention of listening at the door of the séance room. In later years I would pull her leg about this and say that she was nosey!

I imagine she must have been a little bit anxious when, as she leant lightly against the closed door, it opened fractionally. Everybody inside the room was taken aback as all of a sudden a deep and mellifluous voice boomed out, 'Let the child in!' It was the voice of Mrs Duncan's guide, Albert Stuart. The door was duly opened, Heather went in and was allowed to remain for the rest of the séance. It was an experience she would never forget, even if she was reprimanded by her parents afterwards. She sat with

Mrs Duncan on one further occasion, but it was by invitation – she didn't have to creep downstairs that time!

Though some five miles from the British mainland, the Isle of Wight was heavily targeted by the Luftwaffe, particularly in the area of Ventnor. From the German point of view there was an important strategic reason for this. The Downs on the outskirts of Ventnor are very high and had therefore been chosen by the British to house an early-warning radar system which would alert not only the authorities on the Isle of Wight but also those on the mainland when enemy bombers were approaching. Destroying this equipment was thus a high priority for the Germans and Ventnor endured regular onslaughts from their planes.

By 1943 Heather had left school and was apprenticed to a hairdressing salon in Ventnor. The salon was housed in a three-storey building and planes flew over it almost constantly. On one particular day Heather was working on the top floor when, to her great consternation, a German aircraft flew past at the level of the window behind which she was standing. In what must have been a terrifying moment for her, she found herself face to face with the pilot, who then waved to her. Years later, she told me that she had never been so frightened in all her life.

About half an hour after that incident a bomb was dropped nearby, destroying a number of houses. Heather's father was of course extremely concerned about these events and reluctantly came to the decision that for her own safety she must leave the island.

By this time, Heather's brother Dennis, who was serving in the RAF, had married Celia, a lady from Stourbridge in the Midlands. Her father therefore decided Heather should be sent to that area until such time as it was safe for her to return to the Isle of Wight. However, Celia had continued to live with her family after her marriage to Dennis and was unable to accommodate Heather. Thus Heather had no choice but to lodge with three or four different families, which, kind though they were, must have been an unsettling experience at best.

For a young girl to have to leave behind her home and much-loved father in such circumstances was harrowing. Not only was she thrust into a new and unfamiliar life, she also worried constantly about her father, never knowing quite what was happening to him. It was, as she told me later, an experience which had riveted itself upon her memory.

The traumatic events which had brought Heather to the Midlands were to alter the course of her life and my own. She now lived just a few miles from my home and our first meeting was imminent. In one of life's strange but undoubtedly pre-ordained 'coincidences' I decided to join the North Worcestershire Operatic Society, and it was during one of their rehearsals, which were held in Old Swinford church hall, that Heather and I first met.

Chapter 3

Harold Vigurs and Vincent Turvey

I have mentioned that Ernest Oaten conducted the opening ceremony for Heather's father's church at Ventnor and I cannot think of him without recalling a most remarkable incidence of mediumship, told to me by Harold Vigurs, in which he and Ernest Oaten played a role.

Over the years I have been privileged to meet and count as friends a number of exceptional Spiritualists, but few had such an influence upon my own spiritual and philosophical outlook as did Harold.

He was greatly loved by those who knew him, and I likened him to the spiritual teacher Sir George Trevelyan, because they shared the same quiet gentleness and breadth of spiritual understanding. A Home Office solicitor by profession, Harold was an accomplished speaker for the Spiritualist cause and could hold an audience in the palm of his hand. I still have some recordings of lectures that he gave and they are as fresh and relevant today as they were when he first delivered them.

Though he was a dedicated Spiritualist, and served as president of the Spiritualists' National Union between 1943 and 1948, Harold's interest in religion and philosophy was open-minded and wide-ranging, encompassing many avenues of thought, and he had read extensively. Heather and I were fortunate in that he would come and stay with us from time to time and, since his knowledge was tremendous, we learned a great deal from him. Our conversations inspired me and spurred me to embark upon further investigations of my own.

From amongst the many things in which he was interested, he spoke to us at one time of Subud, which he saw as a further avenue for spiritual studies. It was – and still is – an international group of men and women who practise a form of spiritual training known as the latihan – a Thai word meaning exercise. Subud is not a religiously exclusive organisation; it has members from a variety of faiths, including Jews, Christians, Muslims, Buddhists, Spiritualists and even atheists and agnostics. Harold introduced us to a holy man from Indonesia who had been the instigator of the Subud movement and through him we met various others who were involved.

Harold also spoke to me about Hinduism and for a time I involved myself in finding out more about it. I did not make a deep enquiry but did visit a few Hindu temples. I also made a point of looking into Islam, reading the Koran. What it brings to religious dedication and discipline is certainly to be admired.

Harold had widened my horizons and given me a yearning to find out more about many things. Sikhism was another religion which interested me and I spent some time reading their sacred book and involved myself with a number of Sikhs.

I suppose it could be said that I dipped my toe into many different waters. In doing so, I was given the privilege of finding new light on a range of philosophical and religious matters. As a result, I cannot accept that any one religion possesses the sum total of truth, and that is why I think Spiritualism sometimes fails in its true purpose. Each religion or belief system has begun with a single thread, yet that pure thread can become complicated and obscured by the passage of time and lose sight of its connection to the psychic stream.

* * * *

You will forgive me, I hope, if I digress from my own story for a moment to relate what Harold told me.

Few people today will have heard of Vincent Turvey who, to say the least, was a most unusual medium.

I never knew him personally, although I did meet his daughter Dorothy – a gifted medium in her own right.

Vincent's rare type of mediumship – which he termed 'phonevoyance' – enabled him to pick up contacts from spirit people hours before his demonstrations. Those who had benefited from the accuracy of this ability wrote sincere letters of gratitude to him, and also to psychical researchers so that they might be made aware of the work he was doing.

Vincent also possessed another striking gift: the ability to view remotely in great detail.

A particularly good example of this ability occurred when Harold Vigurs and Ernest Oaten were due to take part in a public meeting with Vincent Turvey.

On the morning before the event Harold and Ernest travelled to Bournemouth and were strolling along enjoying the sunshine when both felt a strong inclination to speak with Vincent Turvey.

Telephones were not common at that time, and mobile phones were unheard of, so they went into a nearby shop and asked the proprietor if they might use his phone. He agreed, as long as they paid for the call.

Ernest dialled Vincent's number. After a few seconds the call was answered, and before he had a chance even

Harold Vigurs
President of the SNU 1943-48

to introduce himself a voice at the other end said, 'Hello Oaten. How nice to see you.'

'Nice to see me?' enquired a puzzled Ernest Oaten. 'How can you see me?'

'Well of course I can see you!' responded Turvey.

Bemused, Oaten countered that if Turvey could see him, he should be able to tell him where he, Ernest, was.

Immediately, Turvey replied, 'You are in a greengrocer's shop.'

Bowled over by this, Oaten pressed the medium further: 'If you can see me that clearly, tell me what I am doing now.'

Without hesitation, Turvey replied, 'You are putting your hand on a box of apples.' This was quite correct.

'And what am I doing now?' asked Oaten.

'You are picking up a cabbage,' came the reply, correct again.

Oaten, an extremely perceptive and experienced investigator, was amazed by this exchange and said to Turvey, 'I've got someone here who would like to speak with you.'

'Put Vigurs on,' said Turvey, though Oaten had not named his friend. He passed the phone to Vigurs.

'Nice to see you, Vigurs,' said the medium.

Harold Vigurs was dumbfounded and asked Turvey, 'What am I doing?'

'You're picking up a tomato,' came the reply.

'And what am I touching now?'

'A bunch of grapes,' answered Turvey. Both observations were correct.

At the close of this most unusual conversation Turvey asked Ernest and Harold to visit him for tea before the evening meeting, an invitation they readily accepted.

Arriving at his home, the two men enjoyed the refreshments Turvey offered and then chatted for a while about the earlier greengrocery episode. They were wholly unprepared for Turvey's next statement.

'By the way,' he said, 'I've written down all my evidence for tonight's meeting.'

Ernest and Harold were stunned by this and said in chorus, 'You've what?'

'It's all here,' continued Turvey. He then showed them a piece of paper containing details of chairs and their locations in the demonstration hall, explaining that he would be giving spirit messages to the individuals who would occupy those particular seats.

'But that would be fraud!' said his guests.

Undeterred, Turvey answered, 'Oh no. To me it's just the same as giving a contact at the time.'

Later that evening, with the meeting under way, Ernest Oaten began his address. As he did so, Harold Vigurs, who was chairing the meeting, noticed that there was just one empty chair towards the back of the hall. It remained vacant even as Turvey rose to begin his demonstration.

Telling me later about the events of that day, Harold said to me, 'Eric, at that point I thought to myself: I've got him now. That chair was one to which a message was going to be directed. I'll prove Turvey a fraud!'

But as he explained, no sooner had he entertained this thought than the door opened and in walked a man who sat down on that one vacant chair. Within a few minutes Turvey turned

Ernest Oaten
President of the SNU
1915-20 and 1922-23

to him and gave him a message from his wife in spirit, at which he wept tears of joy as he accepted detail after detail as accurate.

As the meeting reached its conclusion and Ernest Oaten was offering a closing prayer, Harold unobtrusively left the platform and headed towards the man in the vacant chair, who was getting to his feet and preparing to leave. Determined as ever to verify the accuracy of a spirit message, Harold asked him if he had ever before met the medium who had given him this startling evidence of survival.

'No,' answered the man. 'I've never seen him before and I've never been to anything like this before. I was walking past and I just came in on impulse.'

Harold continued to question him closely and asked if he might write to the man in the near future. The man agreed. Harold later told me that their correspondence confirmed that this most extraordinary episode was entirely true. Vincent Turvey was not a professional medium and charged nothing at all for his services.

Harold Vigurs passed in 1972, too soon, it seemed to me, for he was only in his early seventies and had so much more to give. However, it was clearly his time, and I felt the loss of him greatly. I still have some of the letters he sent me and they are a valued reminder of a fine friend.

Chapter 4

A whole new world

A new business venture ✦ *A remarkable séance* ✦ *A proposal* ✦
Married life

1950 was to prove a most significant year in my life, from both professional and personal points of view.

On the first day of November I started a business with two colleagues, Percy Brown and Derek Westlake, whom I had met at Stourbridge church. Drawing on my earlier experience of working as a representative for a stationery firm, we began by selling greeting cards and were modestly successful. Having no premises of our own, we were fortunate in being able to use a cellar belonging to Eric Wright, with whom, as I have already mentioned, I had become friendly through our shared membership of the church.

Eric's family owned a fairly large factory which produced items of bespoke tailoring, making clothes for people in various parts of the world, including Middle Eastern sheikhs and Indian maharajahs. Their business was well respected. The factory's cellar area was extensive, and in those early days we were able to store our stuff and run our business from there. We greatly appreciated Eric's generosity.

Despite the challenges of our new business venture my interest in singing remained as strong as ever, and I continued to perform with the North Worcestershire Operatic Society. Though Heather and I would see each other during rehearsals, and also from time to time at Stourbridge church, we did not at first strike up any particular relationship. We were simply casual acquaintances. Over time a closer friendship developed between us, and as our common interests grew, we would attend circles, lectures, talks and social events within the church as well as at other establishments where, being younger people, we were always made most welcome.

Our mutual interests were not confined solely to learning, important though this was to both of us. We enjoyed visits to the cinema and liked to watch plays and variety shows at the Shakespeare Theatre and many other venues. We were also determined to learn to play better tennis!

From the time we first met, Heather had lived in Hagley. It was an 'upper-class' area of the Stourbridge district, and because of this some of its younger element were known as 'The Hagley Crowd'.

Heather lived with a lady named Florrie Lamb and her two daughters, Sylvia and Annabel, and was treated kindly and well by all of them. On occasion, both daughters would tell me how fellows of Heather's age or thereabouts would turn up in open-top sports cars, or on expensive Harley-Davidson motorcycles, hoping to take her for a spin as a prelude to what they hoped might become a closer relationship. Heather apparently turned them all down politely.

What a contrast these cars and bikes were to my own blue Ford van – a necessity for my business. And what a lucky chap I was and have subsequently been by virtue of her preference for me.

On occasions when I was out late with Heather, my parents would tell me of the incredible psychic awareness of our dog, Floss, a Welsh collie. It seemed that several minutes before I would arrive home, Floss would go to the door and quietly whimper. The whimpering would then continue until I entered the room.

The street in which we lived was off a busy main road, where a stream of vehicles would constantly pass. No doubt there were many blue Ford vans among them, but Floss the dog could distinguish from all of these the one which would shortly be bringing me home. Who says that dogs or other animals are not sensitive? Whatever your own thoughts, before passing judgement take time to read the extensive body of research which has been conducted by respected scientists, such as Dr Rupert Sheldrake, studying the psychic awareness of animals.

* * * *

I have already mentioned that in my teenage years I attended an Anglican church two or three times each Sunday. Listening to and reading with the teachers there, I was intrigued by biblical references to the physical return of various 'dead' persons, such as Moses and Elijah, and of course to Jesus' own appearance to his followers following his crucifixion and subsequent burial. When later I became convinced by the weight of evidence in support of Spiritualism's message of survival, I began to see these biblical events through rather different eyes and was, to say the least, curious as to whether any comparable manifestations were taking place in our own time, within the UK or elsewhere.

Eventually, Heather's and my mutual interest in Spiritualism led us, along with a hundred or so others, to attend a summer school in South Wales organised by Tom and Mabel Hibbs, stalwarts of Spiritualism in that area. As a result of our attendance we were offered the opportunity to join a few other fortunate people at a physical mediumship séance in Cardiff. It was to take place at the home of a couple named Alec and Louie Harris. We had heard that Alec was that rarest of creatures – a materialisation medium – and we relished the chance to be present at one of his sittings.

Where true physical mediumship is concerned, the resulting phenomena can sometimes be so remarkable as to be almost beyond belief. It is therefore vitally important that steps be taken to ensure there can be no possibility of fraudulent activity occurring. Scrupulous checks must be carried out in advance of the séance to ensure the complete integrity of any phenomena which might manifest.

So it was that the ordinary domestic room in which the séance was to be held was subjected to thorough searching and meticulous examination. Windows, floorboards, the room's fittings and single door all came under the scrutiny of Laurence Wilson, a barrister, and his brother Geoffrey, a physicist, under the watchful eye of their father Percy, none of whom had previously met the medium or his wife.

Percy Wilson was a man of great integrity, respected in many fields. In addition to holding a senior position as Principal Assistant Secretary at the Ministry of Transport, he was also editor of *The Gramophone* magazine and the recipient of international awards for his contributions to the field of sound reproduction. Indeed, he counted the great television and electronics pioneer John Logie Baird as a personal friend. Together with two other sitters, these men examined Alec Harris to assure themselves that there were no items concealed about his person. Their searches satisfactorily completed, we took our seats and, amid an atmosphere of excited anticipation, the séance began.

On instruction from Mrs Harris we started to sing in order to raise the vibrations within the room – sometimes deemed a helpful prelude to the production of physical phenomena. Within a short time raps were heard in various parts of the room, often coming from more than one direction at a time. These percussive sounds were followed by the movement of illuminated séance trumpets (metal or cardboard cone-shaped objects usually one to two feet in length) which danced about the room at varying speeds, sometimes slow and graceful, at other times swift and agile. At one point they passed near to us, even touching us lightly before moving upwards to the ceiling.

A short pause followed this remarkable burst of activity, after which a circle guide from the etheric world materialised in physical form and proceeded to welcome us all.

Following this, spirit helpers of differing physical types manifested one after another. Perhaps the most remarkable of these materialisations was that of a female child who stepped from the cabinet and walked freely amongst us. She was of

Tom and Mabel Hibbs

The physical medium Alec Harris
and his wife Louie

course a complete contrast to Alec Harris in every possible respect, he being a little under six feet tall and in early middle age, she a small girl. I should state here that no physical child – female or male – was present in the séance room.

After this spirit child had left us, there followed what was without doubt the most moving and extraordinary part of the séance. One by one, spirit friends materialised and greeted their loved ones who were present in the séance room. It was the greatest of privileges to bear silent witness to the joyful embrace of loved ones reunited, each sitter clearly recognising their own materialised relative or friend and having not the slightest doubt as to their identity.

The impact of this upon Heather and myself was tremendous, to the point of bewilderment. Such profoundly touching reunions were almost beyond belief, yet they happened, providing healing balm to the souls of those who had loved and lost and found again.

Later on, as the séance drew to its close, and in a level of red light which enabled us all to see clearly, an Arab guide materialised in front of us, dressed in traditional Middle Eastern garments. He was joined by a North American Indian, complete with full feathered headdress. Last to appear was the little girl. In a final act of great evidential value, all three remained with us while the curtain of the cabinet opened to reveal the medium Alec Harris in his chair. We watched enthralled and amazed as the North American Indian dissolved towards the floor and disappeared before our very eyes. The Arab guide followed suit, after which the little girl walked behind the cabinet curtain and the séance came to an end. For me, these remarkable revelations not only equalled but surpassed those long ago recorded events of biblical times.

* * * *

As the bond between Heather and myself continued to grow, we loved to go for walks – never more so than when we would wander through the Clent Hills after North Worcestershire Operatic Society rehearsals had finished.

We were often the only ones on the hills, and though by modern standards it might be regarded as slightly strange, we would just sit on some bench or other, holding hands and gazing up at the constellations, marvelling at the immensity of the universe. On reflection, I suppose those were our early moments of meditation together.

I first met Heather's father – 'Pop' as he was known – in 1954. He was suffering from tuberculosis and as a result had had a lung removed and was recovering at a sanatorium on the outskirts of Ventnor. It was a huge place, stretching for a very considerable distance along the coast. He immediately impressed me and, as subsequent events revealed, I must have impressed him too.

In the spring of 1955, Heather and I planned a second journey to visit him at the sanatorium where he was still being treated. There was a very special reason for this visit: I hoped to ask him for Heather's hand in marriage. I suppose this was not strictly necessary and might seem strange today, but I respected him greatly and it was a courtesy that was important to me. First, however, there was an important question to be asked...

On the way to catch the ferry, Heather and I stopped off in the delightful and picturesque village of Broadway, in Worcestershire. As we sat at an open air table drinking coffee, I formally asked Heather if she would marry me, to which she replied, 'Yes, if you will marry me.' I jumped up from my seat, hugged her and planted a kiss on her lips. I suppose this might have been regarded as unseemly behaviour for a public place in those days, particularly in the sedate little village of Broadway. We celebrated our engagement by opening a large box of Terry's All Gold chocolates – not much by today's standards!

Resuming our journey to the Isle of Wight, we arrived to find Heather's father on a bed outside in the sanatorium grounds, taking the fresh sea air, as was the custom for TB patients at that time. I don't think I actually went down on one knee, but after I had asked him if Heather and I could be married, he looked at me with great sincerity and said simply, 'You'll make a good second son for me.' I was quite touched by that. And so Heather and I became engaged and set our wedding date for 27th December that year. As we began to make plans for the big day one of my first and most important decisions was to invite my cousin Richard to be best man.

* * * *

I would suppose that in all our lives there is some person who will have a particularly significant influence upon us. Sometimes that person will be aware of doing so and at other times they will have little or no awareness of their effect.

Richard – known as 'Rich' – is one such person. From my early teens he was a role model for me, not just because of his kind, generous nature, shown in acts of thoughtfulness to my mother and father, my sister Laura and myself, but in his wise observations and guidance, which continue to this day.

As I write, he is 91 years old and still a man of sharp mind, with a tremendous recall of past events and a sound grasp of current affairs.

Rich's kindness knows no bounds. When, as I described in chapter one, my brother Bert was killed, Rich would drive from Birmingham to visit my parents, offering assistance in any way he could. This was at a time of great austerity when petrol was strictly rationed, yet he always managed to find sufficient not only to reach my parents' home but also to take them out into the countryside to bring them some measure of enjoyment which might help to alleviate their sadness.

Later, when I was in hospital in Sleaford, Lincolnshire, and afterwards in the RAF hospital at Cosford following surgery on my spine, he brought my parents to visit me, an act of kindness which greatly helped to ease their anxiety and gave me the pleasure of seeing them – something which lifted my spirits enormously at a difficult time. I shall ever be grateful to him for this, although he would not wish me to be.

Since August 1967 Rich has lived in Douglas, on the Isle of Man, now regrettably on his own after the passing of his wife Joyce, and currently suffering from cancer. Despite all this, and the fact that his three children now live in England, he never complains. He maintains a dignity and poise which cannot fail to impress those who know and love him.

People tell me that his voice and manner of speech are very similar to my own, an observation which pleases me no end, since my respect and affection for him are boundless. Although we are rarely able to see each other now, our telephone conversations bring me great pleasure and have a considerable impact upon me. I could never adequately convey my appreciation of all he has done for me.

* * * *

Our wedding day dawned bright and sunny, the crisp winter air a reminder of the Christmas festivities not long past. As Heather and her father were driven to Stourbridge church I waited inside, as nervous and excited as any bridegroom awaiting the arrival of his bride. My sister Laura acted as Heather's maid of honour and we were a small family group that day, my mother having passed away in 1954 and my father being unable to attend the ceremony because of ill health. I feel certain, though, that they were with us in mind if not in body.

To our delight, Laura, who has a gift for words and has since written many Spiritualist hymns, wrote a special one for the occasion. Sung to the tune of *Smiling Through*, it began with the verse:

In your presence oh God we assemble this day
To commend these two souls to your care;
To unite them in love
May your light from above
Shed its golden ray on each fresh day they share.

*Heather arrives at the
church with her father*

*Cutting the cake takes
great concentration*

December 27th 1955 – Our Wedding Day

The service was conducted by Mabel Hibbs, whom we had come to know and love so well through our attendance at the Welsh summer schools. Mabel's beloved husband Tom had passed away not long before and, looking back, it must have been a very poignant experience for her to conduct our wedding ceremony. Nevertheless, she did so wonderfully and when it came to signing the registers our friend Albert Taylor performed his role as authorised person.

After the ceremony we held a reception at The White Horse restaurant – a very happy event attended by family and many friends from the worlds of Spiritualism, business and music. In addition to the traditional speeches, several guests made kind and complimentary remarks about both of us, one or two taking advantage of the opportunity to throw in a few rather humorous quips about me! Heather and I were enjoying the reception so much that we had to be reminded to go and change out of our wedding clothes in order to catch a train from Birmingham's Snow Hill Station to London, where we were to begin our honeymoon.

When Heather emerged from the changing room she looked stunning, dressed in a lovely two-piece winter suit with hat and gloves to complete the effect. I was overwhelmed by the picture she made, as shouts of admiration went up from the assembled guests. My memories of that moment remain vivid to this day.

The car which would take us to Birmingham was ready and waiting, and our guests followed us outside to give us a cheerful send-off. Heather and I climbed inside, as did my business partner, Percy Brown. This caused much amusement to some of our younger guests, and a shout went up, followed by a number of mischievous comments, such as 'Do you need to be chaperoned then, Eric?'

As we took our leave and drove away amidst heaps of good wishes, I noticed out of the corner of my eye that some of our friends were getting into an old car. I thought no more about it until we arrived at the station. There, lining up, was the crowd of friends who had evidently raced ahead in order to get there before us. They proceeded to escort us down onto the platform and watched as we boarded the train to London, accompanied by... Percy!

Oh, what shouts and ribbing erupted from the crowd! 'Never thought you'd both need a chaperone!' called one. 'Need someone to show you the ropes?' teased another. What a send-off it was – although I am not sure Heather enjoyed it too much, especially when various other passengers on the train began to join in!

The truth of the matter was that Percy had travelled up from London to attend our wedding and was now returning to continue the holiday he had been enjoying with Derek and some other old friends. Since trains to London were so few and far between he'd had no alternative but to catch the same one as we did!

Arriving in the big city, we checked in to a pleasant hotel in Southampton Row and over the next few days took the opportunity to visit a number of places of mutual interest, among them the British Museum, the Tower of London, the Tate Gallery and Buckingham Palace, little realising that decades later we would be invited to this last as guests at one of the Queen's garden parties. We also attended several theatres, taking particular pleasure in watching Richard Attenborough's performance in Agatha Christie's famous play, *The Mousetrap*.

Leaving London, we continued on to Norwich to stay with our friend Norman Morris who was deputy head of music at the well-respected independent Norwich School. We had a fine time and shared many joyous musical interludes while we were there.

Afterwards, Heather took me to meet some of her relatives who were living on farms in the countryside close to Norwich. I suppose they were keen to size up her new husband, since they all thought a great deal of her and wanted to make sure I was good enough!

Returning from our honeymoon we were eager to settle down to married life and shortly afterwards moved into a flat which had been created over the top of the business premises my partners and I had bought in 1951 in Upper High Street, Cradley Heath, after outgrowing the cellar space so kindly loaned to us by Eric Wright.

Derek Westlake had worked all kinds of hours to make it ready for us and had done a splendid job. The flat was a fair size and had the added bonus of a long back garden which contained some fine old apple trees. Those apples tasted as good as any I have ever eaten and we had orange boxes full of them once they were ready to pick.

After we had settled in I arranged for a removal firm to bring my piano from my father's home, but what should have been a simple delivery turned out to be a bit more complicated than I had expected...

It seemed I had not done my calculations as well as I should have. To get the piano up into the flat the removal men had not only to remove the window in the kitchen, but also the entire window frame.

However, as time went by the difficulty we had in getting the piano into our front room more than paid off, for in the months and years that followed we had some wonderful musical evenings when my friends Norman Morris, Leslie Sykes, Arthur Woodall and Charles Badham would play piano accompaniments for myself and several of my singing pals, including Harry Millward, Cecil Drew, Frank Baker, Sheila Marshall and Betty Chandler, who had been a professional opera singer.

Betty and her husband ran the famous Buddle Inn near Ventnor and whenever they came over to see Heather's dad – who by then had moved to the mainland and was living with his son Dennis in Stourbridge – a 'must' on their visiting list was Upper High Street, Cradley Heath, for the hours of musical pleasure we would all enjoy together. Between us, we covered a whole range of styles – from opera, oratorio and lieder to ballads and show songs, with some Old Tyme Music Hall numbers thrown in for good measure. I could never have imagined that my old upright piano would become the source of so many wonderful musical moments.

After we had been in our flat for a while, Heather and I decided that we must try to put some covering on the bare floorboards in our bathroom. Money was tight, but somehow we scraped together enough to buy some lino. I measured carefully around the pedestals and bath, making sure I would get just enough lino but not too much, and then set off for the local carpet shop.

The owner regarded me with undisguised astonishment as I presented him with my precisely worked out diagram and calculations. 'You'd better go back and recheck them,' he said, 'or you might be three or four inches out.'

I duly returned to the bathroom, rechecked my figures and went back to the shop. 'Look, lad,' said the long-suffering owner, 'I'll give you six inches more free of charge.'

Back at the flat, Heather and I set about laying the new lino and, after an hour or two of careful cutting and fitting, stood up and looked with pride at our handiwork. As I reflected on the purchase, I guessed that the shop owner must have thought me a right chump, but we needed to economise and I didn't care.

Chapter 5

Triumphs and troubles

An intriguing prediction • The sweet sound of success • International Spiritualism comes to London • Messing about on the river • A new family member • Troubled times for the SNU • A technical hitch...

I have already referred to the gifted medium Walter Brooks, and in early 1957 he came to stay with Heather and myself. He was an uneducated lad from Yorkshire and hadn't got two pennies to rub together, but when he spoke from the platform his choice of words and his phraseology were something to be admired. When he demonstrated it was with a clarity and accuracy almost equal to Gordon Higginson's. Walter was a humble person, and if he could take a service and receive a small stipend at the end of it, he was happy. He was quite content to do what he did, reuniting people with their loved ones.

As we sat chatting one day, he asked Heather if she was thinking of having a baby. 'No, not really,' she replied. 'We might at some time.'

Walter persisted, saying, 'Well, I think you will and it may not be all that long. I think it will be a boy, and I think he will be born on 6th December.'

Well, there was no sign of this, but as time went by Heather had cause to visit the doctor, who confirmed that she was pregnant. The doctor expected that the baby would be born in December.

My musical friend Norman Morris, although never overly critical, was always pulling my leg about Spiritualism. But because we were such good friends, and Heather and I were so excited, I told him about the pregnancy and Walter's prediction. As the months passed he would say to me, 'Eric – it won't be long now. It won't be long till the *boy* comes along!'

By early December it had reached the point where he was ringing me almost every day. 'How are things?' he would ask. 'Has the baby come yet?' By this time I was getting embarrassed because of Walter's prediction. Well, on 17th December not a boy, but Lisa, was born. So much for the prediction!

Needless to say, Norman had great fun teasing me about the fact that we had a daughter and not a son, but for all his good natured banter he was absolutely delighted for us. However, the mystery of Walter's seemingly quite inaccurate prediction was to remain unsolved for some time...

With my good friend Norman Morris

The first four years of Lisa's life were spent at the flat. Her presence in our lives was a great joy to us and we lavished loving care on her. Being such a pretty child, she drew admiring glances and compliments from many people in Cradley Heath as Heather pushed her in her lovely big pram – a gift from my business partner Percy.

* * * *

Despite the demands of family life, a growing business and, of course, my work for Spiritualism, I was determined to continue with my passion for singing. By this time I had met up with many musical people, some of whom seemed to feel that my voice had real potential. One in particular, who had a very good voice and certainly more experience than I, had persuaded me to transfer to his own singing teacher in Birmingham, a man named Albert Knight. Albert was a kindly man, and liked to encourage his pupils to enter for singing competitions. I was not successful in all those I entered, but I certainly was in quite a number of them.

Of course, in preparation for the competitions I had to learn some difficult songs and on a number of occasions I would either win first prize or be commended for receiving high marks. Unfortunately, since the repertoire was largely classical – lovely music – it couldn't necessarily be used in concerts because very few people were appreciative of it. Thus I added other styles to my repertoire, including comic opera and ballads. I continued to be in contact with a number of pals who were musically inclined, particularly Norman Morris. He was a very talented pianist and eventually went on to train some fine choral groups, becoming quite famous for his work with the Reading Phoenix Choir. He would arrange all manner of music for them and was so respected by some well-known composers that they would write music especially for his choir to première.

In 1960 I entered the International Eisteddfod, a major singing competition held at Llangollen in Wales. I had previously won various semi-Eisteddfods but this particular one was a far tougher affair and I was thrilled to be awarded first prize in the tenor solos. Of the two songs I sang, one was compulsory – the famous *Nessun Dorma* from Puccini's opera, *Turandot*. The other piece, my own choice, was *Silent Noon*, a hauntingly beautiful song by the English composer, Ralph Vaughan Williams.

* * * *

Within weeks I was singing again at an event of a very different kind, as Spiritualists from almost thirty countries converged on London for the Triennial Congress of the International Spiritualist Federation.

The weather was particularly fine during the seven-day gathering and delegates from Australia, Belgium, Canada, Denmark, Egypt, Finland, France, Germany, Holland, India, Italy, Northern and Southern Ireland, Kenya, Mexico, New Zealand, Norway, Portugal, Puerto Rico, Scotland, South Africa, Spain, Sweden, Switzerland, Turkey, the USA, Wales and, of course, England, basked in the unexpected but welcome warmth of an English late summer.

Lectures, talks, and demonstrations of mediumship and healing were held in various large halls and other venues across London. The Connaught Rooms, Victoria Hall, St. Pancras Town Hall and Caxton Hall were all pressed into service as some of the finest mediums and speakers of the day enthralled and inspired the many international visitors. Prime among the speakers was Air Chief Marshal Lord Dowding, who formally welcomed the delegates to London on behalf of the ISF.

I had the honour of singing at the opening banquet in the Connaught Rooms on Saturday 10th September. It was a vibrant and colourful affair, with many delegates dressed in national costume. Guests of honour were the Danish medium Einer Nielsen and Dr and Mrs James F. Malcolm. Dr Malcolm was a distinguished scientist specialising in agricultural bacteriology who had become a SNU minister on his retirement. I also sang at other venues during the congress week, on one occasion performing a Swedish song. This delighted the Swedish contingent, who told me they were friends of the famous tenor Jussi Björling and that the song I had sung was one of his favourites. On their return home to Sweden they kindly sent me copies of a number of other Swedish songs, in some cases autographed by Jussi himself.

One of these ladies, named Marie Louise, was so impressed by Walter Brooks' evidential demonstration of mediumship (he was able to relay some details to her in Swedish) that she invited him to visit Sweden and stay in her family home. Her husband was a high court judge and when Walter eventually arrived there the couple took him to a castle

Entertaining the audience with some songs from my repertoire

they owned in the north of Sweden. I have always been intrigued by something Walter told me about that trip. Walter was, if I may use the term, a 'cold bird', for he had a real problem with chilly weather and usually wore at least one and sometimes two pullovers when he came to stay with us. However, the cold air of northern Sweden had been a different matter altogether, and had provided him with a new and fascinating insight into his own mediumship. In that crisp, rarefied air the clarity of his clairaudience was apparently almost 100 per cent sharper than normal.

In another demonstration to congress delegates, a further interesting aspect of Walter's mediumship was revealed when he directed a message to a Spanish lady and her daughter who, respectively, had lost their husband and father. Walter had no knowledge of any language other than English so the information was relayed through an interpreter. Suddenly, and completely without warning, Walter broke into Spanish, astounding everyone present, none more so than the two Spanish ladies themselves. The husband in spirit was telling the two ladies through Walter that he knew they had had to lie in order to attend the congress, saying that they were coming to England for a conference on herbal medicine. The reason for this deception was that the Spanish dictator General Franco held the country in an iron grip and Spiritualism had been outlawed by his regime.

In addition to the outstanding demonstrations given by Walter, the congress week was packed with other exceptional mediumship and oratory, with demonstrations by British mediums Ena Twigg, William Redmond and Doris Adams. Americans Keith Rhinehart, Dorothy Smith and Evelyn Muse also demonstrated, as did French medium Lucienne Lemaire. An impressive array of speakers included Percy Wilson, Maurice Barbanell and Richard Ellidge from England, the South African Edward Bentley, German Theodor Weimann and Walter-Joseph Donnay of Belgium. Subjects covered by the various speakers were wide-ranging, reflecting the vibrant Spiritualist movement of the day. The Spirit State of Existence, The Mission of Spiritualism, Paranormal Phenomena and Contemporary Society, The Ideology of Spiritualism, The Tragedies of Mediumship, Psychic Development Techniques, The Future of Spiritualism – these were just some of the topics covered, most ending with a lively question-and-answer discussion forum.

Towards the end of the week delegates were taken by coach to Shere in Surrey, home of the Harry Edwards Healing Sanctuary at Burrows Lea. Once there, they were entertained to tea by the famous healer and his two associates, George and Olive Burton.

The ISF's Triennial Congress was seen as a resounding success, a marvellous feat of organisation on the part of the committee, ably led by its chairman Mabel Hibbs. The whole week left me and, I'm sure, the other delegates, with wonderful memories.

* * * *

The International Eistedfodd and the congress had occupied much of my time, both in preparation and participation, and some leisure time was called for. Much against their better judgement I persuaded our friends Jim and Pat Higgs to join Heather and myself in a hired rowing boat on the River Severn at Bewdley, in Worcestershire. I was to pay for my persuasive ways a short time later...

The Severn is a fairly fast-flowing and deep river, and to get down to it at Bewdley you have to descend many steps. Only as we clambered somewhat clumsily into the boat, and Jim and I each took a pair of oars, did the ladies realise that neither of us knew how to row! Nevertheless, we managed to move away from the landing stage into midstream, our complete lack of rhythm causing considerable splashing of water into the boat. This was bad enough in itself, but when we had managed somehow to travel a distance upstream, we tried to turn the boat around, our amateur efforts being so inept that they seriously frightened Pat, Heather and even Jim himself. Eventually we managed to get the boat to face the other direction, but by this time all four of us were soaked to the skin.

Putting a brave face on it, we headed back downstream, but to our horror the heavens opened and it started to pour with rain. I urged everyone to keep calm, trying my utmost to assure them that we would be all right. Eventually we reached the landing stage and somehow climbed out of the boat, by which time we were all four completely drenched and extremely grateful to be on dry land again.

Both ladies reprimanded me very considerably for persuading them and Jim to go on a boat when I was no rower, but as I told them at the time – you have to experiment with life, otherwise it would be very dull!

* * * *

In 1961 Heather became pregnant for a second time and we were both delighted at the prospect of having another child. She had given birth to Lisa in hospital, but since all had gone according to plan on that occasion and this would be her second delivery, a home birth was decided upon.

Shortly before Lisa's fourth birthday, it became clear that Heather had gone into labour, and though I tried my best to be helpful I was nevertheless ordered by the midwife, and our very dear friend Polly who was assisting Heather, to get out of the flat and not return until I was called back. I was very anxious about not being able to do anything to help, and paced the lounge restlessly. After a while I went down to the warehouse but could not settle to doing any work, though there was certainly plenty of it to be done.

Pacing anxiously again, I opened the front door onto the road and saw a policeman from the nearby station passing by. I knew him quite well and he stopped to talk. I explained that Heather was giving birth to our second child and that I had been exiled for the time being. He was clearly a little concerned and said, 'Come to the station with me and I'll make you a cup of tea.' It was a kind offer but I declined it and went back inside. Feeling increasingly anxious and helpless, I went to the bottom of the stairs and called, 'May I come up? Is everything all right?' I was told to calm down and go into the garden, which, having no alternative, I did.

Heaven knows how long I walked up and down that garden, but at approximately 7.30am on 6th December I was summoned by Polly to come and meet my new baby son. I could not hold back the tears as I raced up the stairs and into the bedroom, where I first embraced Heather and was then handed my little son, Jonathan, by the midwife. Words could never describe what that moment meant to me. How different my experience was by comparison with more modern times, when partners are actively encouraged to be present at the birth of their children.

Since Walter Brooks had given us the date of 6th December four years earlier and told us we would have a boy, as the anxiety and excitement of the preceding hours began to fade, my brain started to work, pondering the question of how such specific predictions can from time to time be fulfilled. The business of times and dates from the spirit world's perspective has always intrigued me. It seems that we get an overlapping of time in the clairvoyant facility which, in some people's opinions, is all happening at that one moment. Whilst this may to some extent be true, it suggests to me – as it has to researchers far more learned than I – that it all belongs to the 'now'. By that I mean that events of the past, of today and of the future are all part of an extension of time as we know it. In his book *An Experiment With Time*, published in 1927, the scientist John William Dunne postulates this theory and makes a very convincing case for it.

Walter Brooks would have had to interpret the information he received clairvoyantly or clairaudiently, as would any other medium. Whilst we, and no doubt the mediums themselves, might wish the process of communication to be akin to a telephone call, it is not so, and the mechanics of it are far from straightforward. Whatever the case, Walter was a fine medium and I have always thought it a pity that he was not more widely recognised.

* * * *

On a cold winter's day a few weeks after Jonathan's birth we moved into our first real home – a house in Castle Grove, Stourbridge. It was a nice house with a pleasant garden which had a stream running through it. One section of the garden, on the far side of the stream, was completely inaccessible, so, aided by the strength and determination of one of my musical pals, Bill Skidmore, I decided to build a bridge across the stream using heavy old railway sleepers. Our own two children and hosts of their young friends were thrilled and took great delight in playing games over that makeshift bridge. To this day they can recall what happy times they had.

Once we had settled into our new home, one of our first decisions was to invite Heather's father – 'Pop' – to come and live with us. I had considerable affection and respect for him and was delighted that he and I would now have the opportunity to enjoy regular conversations. Our talks always inspired me, for, as I mentioned in chapter two, he was a dedicated Spiritualist and had a wealth of knowledge and experience, along with an open mind and a unique outlook on many things that were of interest to me.

Once Pop was with us he would often look after the children when Heather and I were out. One Sunday night Walter Brooks was serving our church. After the service we hurried home, knowing that Pop planned to take Walter out for a drink.

Together, they set off for the Seven Stars, just a few minutes away from our house. Being a Sunday night, the pub was packed with local railway employees and their wives, and a pianist was entertaining them.

As Walter sat sipping his beer, a strange expression passed across his face and Pop asked him what was the matter.

'There's somebody here but I've told them I've finished my demonstration for the night,' Walter answered. He took another sip of his drink, but it seemed the spirit person was reluctant to take no for an answer.

Giving in, Walter said, 'I can't tell if it's a man or a woman, but they're wearing a large-rimmed black hat and a cloak.' Deciding it was a man, he continued, 'He says he knew you when you were in the East End of London. You went up to him in a pub and asked if you could have the pleasure of buying him a drink.'

Walter added that the man was explaining that he and Pop later shared drinks on a number of occasions and became firm friends. He concluded, 'Now he's taking off his hat, holding it in one hand and swirling the cloak with the other. He's bowing slightly and saying he's G.K. Chesterton.'

Pop confirmed that he had been friendly with Chesterton, who passed in 1936. It was remarkable evidence, delivered through a tired medium in a noisy pub.

* * * *

Family life suffered an unpleasant blow when, at just two years old, Jonathan was taken ill with measles. It was a severe attack, which caused him real distress and concerned Heather and myself greatly. Christmas was upon us, and the prospect of lying in bed feeling ill was a bitter disappointment for a little boy, who, like all children, had been extremely excited about the impending festivities. Nevertheless, that was what the doctor had ordered, and in a darkened room, to make matters worse. Being so small, Jonathan couldn't understand why this was necessary and became all the more upset on Boxing Day when Heather and I had to go downstairs to prepare food for my special cousin Rich and his wife Joyce, who would shortly be arriving with their children.

Rich was an optician and had his own business in Hereford. He well knew how serious and unpleasant measles could be for a small child, and as a result spent almost the whole day in Jonathan's bedroom, holding his hand, talking to him and trying to keep him calm. I will never forget that devotion to my son, the more so because it was Boxing Day, and Rich had looked forward to spending it with us.

When Jonathan had recovered, he was left with a significant squint in one eye, which caused concern to Heather and myself. We sought medical advice, only to be told there was little or nothing that could be done. When he was three, we made the decision to take him to the well-known healer George Chapman, to see if his spirit control,

George Chapman and his son Michael, also a healer

Dr Lang, could do anything to help. His intervention was successful, and we returned home with the problem corrected. Though Jonathan has worn glasses ever since, the squint has never returned.

It was not until years later that we met George Chapman again, when we attended a function at a hotel in Stratford-upon-Avon to celebrate his many years of dedication as a healer. Though we chatted with him about Jonathan's healing, he had no recollection of it, having been in trance and under the control of Dr Lang. He was an unassuming person and took no personal credit for the cure.

We were always exceedingly close to our children, as they were to us. When they were very young we would frequently have people to stay with us in Castle Grove, usually mediums and speakers who had come for the weekend to serve our church. Harold Vigurs, Gordon Higginson, Mary Duffy, Albert Best, Doris Collins, Coral Polge, Jill Harland and Gerard Smith were just a few amongst the dozens to whom we gave hospitality over the years.

There was one aspect of Heather's wonderful hospitality with which I frequently disagreed, because I was concerned that she should not exhaust herself. No matter how late it was when we retired for the night, she would always insist on laying the table in readiness for the next morning's breakfast. She would often be extremely tired by this time but she would never be dissuaded from performing this thoughtful courtesy for whoever was staying with us.

Heather with Jonathan and Lisa

Lisa was quite bright at school but we found that Jonathan had some slight difficulties. What we didn't realise at the time was that he had dyslexia. Some years earlier I had become interested in the Rudolf Steiner Society and its principles, and it may well have been that interest which prompted me to send Jonathan to a school in Love Lane, Stourbridge, modelled on those same principles. For a year or two he was quite happy there, but as time went by we felt that if we were sending him to a private school we should really do the same for Lisa. Since we had a good local school for Lisa we decided to send Jonathan there too. In spite of the fact that he has always had a mild degree of dyslexia, he is very bright and has done extremely well.

* * * *

Spiritualism continued to be a driving force in our lives and in 1962 I was elected president of Stourbridge church, with which I had been closely associated since that first dramatic evidence of my brother's survival, given to me by Gordon Higginson in 1947.

I also continued to sing, and was never more delighted than when an opportunity arose to combine my music with my Spiritualism. One such occasion, memorable for reasons which will become embarrassingly obvious, was in 1965 when I was invited to sing at the opening ceremony of Edward Street Church in Brighton.

The building was most unusually designed and an artist had been engaged to create items of glass to grace its interior. One of these was suspended from the ceiling and was very much a centrepiece, since lights were played upon it.

As the packed congregation listened attentively to what one person later described as the 'lilt' of my voice, panic suddenly ensued as I hit a high note and parts of that remarkable glass creation shattered into pieces! Fortunately, no one was hurt as it crashed to the floor.

I was not invited to sing there for some years afterwards. I wonder why...

After three or four years I was restored to favour and invitations were extended to Heather and myself at fairly regular intervals. They continued until the passing of the church's president, Ivor Davies, whose funeral service I conducted.

By this time I had become increasingly involved in Spiritualism at a national level and, as a result, was closely connected with Stansted Hall from 1966 onwards. Arthur Findlay had kindly bequeathed his magnificent home to the Spiritualists' National Union in 1964 and ever since then I have had a great love for the place. This might well have been because of its being a grand Hall, which in my wildest dreams I never imagined that the Spiritualist movement could come to own. Yet, in spite of the almost awesome appeal of the building and its extensive grounds, it had unforeseen problems which would gradually come to light as consideration was given to its future use as a college which would accommodate and train students.

In his latter years, particularly following the death of his wife, Gertrude, Mr Findlay had been content to live there in his own long-accepted way, and in the process had failed to maintain or update much of its internal and external structure. There was therefore an urgent need for attention to these matters – a source of great concern to those who were in office at its handover and in the years immediately following. Mr Findlay's gift of his remarkable home had been most generous, but alas he had not provided a sufficient endowment to carry out the remedial work which was so urgently needed.

In order for this work to begin, money had to be taken from the Union's Building Fund Pool – the forerunner of the present SNU Trust. These funds had been provided by churches, not only as an investment, but more especially to assist other churches in carrying out necessary improvements and repairs, since at that time banks would not grant mortgages or any kind of financial advances to our

J.Arthur Findlay O.B.E.

*Stansted Hall: the home of Arthur Findlay which was
bequeathed to the SNU
(This watercolour is by Alan Stuttle who is a tutor at the college)*

movement. However, this withdrawal of funds from the Pool was a source of great concern to many SNU members and created rumours of impending bankruptcy, not only of the Fund but of the Union itself.

The consequent panic which spread within the SNU led to severe criticism of those on the Union's council, and downright insults were directed towards those who had made the decisions. The general atmosphere was tense and nervous, with language unbecoming to its users being voiced at a number of meetings I attended. How the council members withstood these attacks I shall never know, but with hindsight I trust that I and many of those critics will now pay tribute to the early volunteers who worked tirelessly at all kinds of jobs to make the Hall habitable. Electricians, plumbers, decorators, cleaners all willingly pitched in.

In those early days the college programmes were very modest by today's standards, as were the student numbers, and the income was most certainly insufficient to meet the bills. Many lecturers and demonstrators of the time were generous and did not charge for their work; amongst them were Betty and Jack Wakeling and of course the inspirational Gordon Higginson. I cannot but wonder if the college would

Spiritualist Lyceum Week at the Hall 1967

even exist today, had it not been for these and others like them who sacrificed so much to keep the dream alive.

* * * *

Meanwhile, our business continued to thrive and expand. We had enlarged our premises in Cradley Heath and eventually came to the conclusion that we should add a further building at the back. Rather frustratingly, the local council objected to our plan, saying that they were proposing to develop the area and our building ambitions were not consistent with their own plans. By this time Percy Brown had passed away, so Derek and I applied to move on to an estate. This, too, brought objections; we were told that the area in question was for industrial purposes and not for our kind of business.

Well, I suppose I must have been such a pest to them that they finally conceded and in 1967 we were given permission to build a prefabricated structure. Our builder began by installing the necessary drainage, water pipes and heaven knows what else, then laid the brickwork and concrete floor. The building itself was then erected. All this was done in association with the council's building inspectors, who came and measured everything out so it was all in the right place. We had almost reached the long-awaited day of occupation when along came two men who told us that there was something wrong.

'You've built it in the wrong place!' they told us.

'No we haven't!' I said.

The exchange developed into quite an argument and eventually the men went away and returned with their drawings. I had our builder with me by then, and he was capable of reading technical drawings very well. Together we were able to prove to the inspectors that they were wrong. In effect, what they wanted us to do was to uplift the building and move it another few feet. It was ridiculous. Local authorities!

By the time we had been there for twenty months the business was thriving. We had taken on a number of representatives and greatly expanded the range of goods we stocked. We now sold a wide variety of stationery, gift wrap (found in every greeting card shop nowadays, but much rarer then), writing implements such as Parker pens, and a wide selection of balloons, which had by then become very big business. All seemed set fair. Unfortunately, though of course we did not know it at the time, things were about to change.

Chapter 6

Truth will out

Disaster upon disaster ✦ *A sherry, sir?* ✦ *A queen and a medium* ✦
A shameful cover-up

Even with the happiness of living at Castle Grove events determined that we should move on. Heather's father, Pop, was living with us and the children needed separate bedrooms, but even as we were looking around for some larger place we could afford, Pop had a stroke and died within a few hours. As I have already said, he was a lovely man who influenced my life significantly and taught me much. We greatly missed his physical presence with us.

The following year we packed our clothes and other essential items in readiness for our regular pilgrimage to the South Wales summer school in Penarth. We locked up the house, went to notify the police of our departure, and set off in the bright sunshine and warmth of midday. Our good cheer was to be short lived. On the following day Dennis, Heather's brother, contacted us to say that our house had been flooded, the result of a cloudburst, a severe summer storm. The stream bed in our garden had become blocked with rubble from a building

Willie 'Pop' Jermy

site upstream, and the grille gate which I would normally have opened could not cope with the deluge.

Heather and I returned the next day to find the ground floor of our home completely ruined. Parquet flooring, carpets and other possessions were floating in the water that remained. We both felt that we should repair the house and try to restore the happy atmosphere that had existed there, while at the same time starting to look for another house, perhaps a bit bigger.

After viewing a number of properties we set our hearts on a detached house in Broughton Road, Stourbridge, and made an offer to buy it, little knowing that events beyond our control would very soon force us to withdraw from the sale.

In the small hours of 6th December 1969, I was awoken by the shrill ringing of the telephone beside the bed. Reaching sleepily for the receiver I answered the call and was jolted instantly into full consciousness by the words, 'Your building is on fire – you had better come quickly!' My heart racing, I jumped out of bed, hastily threw on some clothes and drove over there like a madman. The building was ablaze. In my state of shock, I did a foolish thing and drove over the fire hoses, eliciting curses from the firemen. I was desperate to get into the building to see if I could save anything and they were rightly furious with me for that. Abandoning the futile attempt, I crossed to the other side of the road and sheltered under the canopy of a nearby factory whose staff I knew. The rain had begun to fall and I stood there silently, watching everything we had worked for go up in smoke. It was not an experience I will ever forget.

The fire brigade had told me that there was nothing I could do, and after speaking with Heather I decided to make my way home. She was as distressed as I was but pointed out that I must come home because it was Jonathan's birthday. A number of children had been invited to his party and they were all looking forward to my being there, she said. So, having spent much of the night and morning confronting the wreckage of our business, in the afternoon I had no alternative but to entertain the children as though nothing at all was amiss. Looking back, it was probably the best means of overcoming the shock of what had happened.

Throughout that afternoon I was pestered, both over the phone and in person, by people wanting to act on our behalf against the insurance company. Some were extremely persistent, ringing three or four times, and I became a bit annoyed, telling them that when I had made up my mind I would let them know. Our insurance agent was a friend of Derek and myself, and told me, 'Eric, it's not for me to say, and it may seem that I'm going against you as friends, but I don't know whether I would go down that route because we have our own assessor.' He explained that the assessor's name was Burton, that he had a reputation for high standards and was extremely strict. He was apparently not the type to stand any nonsense from anybody.

I don't know whether it was because I was so upset, or perhaps because of an instinct, but I didn't go with any of these fellows and instead met Mr Burton myself on the following Monday. I could see straight away that he was a competent man and wouldn't be messed about. He was the sort of person who would go through everything in meticulous detail.

During my interviews with him I was questioned extensively about all manner of things pertaining to the business, the building and the stock, and when it was all over we rebuilt the place in a matter of three or four months – perhaps too quickly, now I reflect back on it, because winter temperatures soon revealed that we had not installed sufficient insulation in the walls and roof. A while after the initial interviews, Mr Burton came to see me and informed me that the insurers and fire officers were still unable to establish exactly what had caused the blaze. He also delivered the depressing news that we had been under-insured, adding that we would therefore receive only a portion of our losses. I told him that I hadn't realised this. After a moment he looked me straight in the eye and said, 'I'll tell you what I'm going to do: I deal with hundreds of people and you've been the most honest man I've ever dealt with. I'm going to put in a full report telling them to pay you everything that is due.' And that is exactly what he did.

The fire had broken out on Friday night/Saturday morning and on the Sunday afternoon, twenty months after moving out, we had sold our old premises – the former café in Upper High Street. On the very day of the fire I had gone to the solicitor's just around the corner from us and signed the papers turning the former café over to the council. In turn, they had made payment just a few hours later. On the Sunday morning I had approached the local mayor, who had previously been to the premises, and who had done some personal insurance work for us, and he told me that he had spoken to one of the officers and they had agreed that we should be allowed to go into our old premises, though they had long been vacant and no electricity or water were connected. Go in, he told me, and we'll see if we can help you.

I don't know how the news of our plight got around, but within three or four hours some of our customers had turned up with buckets and brooms. Among them were Roy Biggs and his wife Joyce, who ran a busy business. Sunday was their one day off, yet they had turned up and worked like Trojans, as did half-a-dozen other people.

On the Monday morning I contacted a firm we dealt with in Northampton and on hearing what had happened to us they were quite upset. Their sales manager was a fairly good friend of ours and he said that they were not going to let us fail. Sure enough, on Monday afternoon at four o'clock, a big vehicle pulled up in front of our building, filled with loads of stuff that we needed.

Some time after we moved back into the offices at the front of the warehouse, which had been largely undamaged by the fire, though of course the carpets and other fittings had been ruined, Mr Burton called to see me.

'You need some new carpet here,' he said.

I told him I couldn't afford it – indeed I was nowhere near being able to afford it.

'We'll manage for a while,' I said to him.

'You might manage,' he said, 'but I'm not going to let you.'

He went on to say that in one of the fires he had recently assessed there had been a quantity of carpet which had come back to him because it had been written off.

'I'd like you to have it,' he said. 'It's a top quality Axminster.'

So he brought it along and we carpeted the entire offices. He wouldn't take a penny for it, and I have never ceased to appreciate his kindness.

A few months later the cause of the fire had still not been established. Gordon Higginson came down to visit and went carefully around the warehouse. After a while, he said to me, 'Eric, I think the fire started here.' What he didn't know was that, since the fire, we had changed around the places where we stored the various items. The fire had spread rapidly, Gordon said, what with the balloons and so on. He added that he thought one of our members of staff had had something to do with what had taken place. This was interesting, since, as we always worked on Saturday mornings, the staff had arrived on the day following the fire, because most of them did not know it had happened. However, one employee, Trevor, did not turn up. I only found that out afterwards, because it wasn't significant at the time.

Trevor, it transpired later, had been down on his luck and must have got into the premises by the side door. That was the entrance for accepting and dispatching goods and we later discovered that the door and locks had been tampered with. Trevor never admitted to any of this but within a week or two of the fire he decided to leave. I think his conscience must have troubled him.

Some time later I spoke again to Mr Burton and a couple of the fire officers, and put that possible scenario to them. They agreed that it was conceivable and that Trevor might have started the fire to cover his tracks, perhaps intending to steal money or goods to relieve his straitened financial circumstances. It was Gordon who established that.

* * * *

In March 1970 we started to move back into the rebuilt warehouse. Our loyal staff, including my secretary Cissie Shaw, representatives Jack Faulkner, Len Lloyd and Heather's brother Dennis Jermy, our greeting card buyer Maureen Willets and Mark Smith our warehouse assistant, were engaged in filling great rows of racking with new merchandise, and to thank them for their efforts and loyalty, and also to keep them warm and in good spirits, I brought along a couple of bottles of wine and a bottle of sherry.

In the late afternoon, when their lessons had finished, Heather went to collect Lisa and Jonathan from school and brought them back to the warehouse. They were keen to help with the restocking, and having shown them what to do, I left them to it, since it seemed they could do no harm and would enjoy the experience.

After about an hour, Joe Davies, our trusted manager, asked me where Jonathan was. I was unsure, and told him to look around and see if he could find him. A few minutes later Joe came back to me, looking a bit agitated.

'Gaffer,' he said, 'you'd better come with me.'

Not knowing what to expect, I followed him, only to find Jonathan – then aged eight – spread-eagled on the floor clutching the almost empty sherry bottle and looking distinctly the worse for wear! I lifted him up and carried him to Heather's car. Shortly afterwards she drove him home. Lisa, who was four years older than Jonathan, was not very pleased with him. Obviously, the experience had a profound and salutary effect on him because to this day he has never touched another drop of sherry!

Though Jonathan felt none too well after his adventure with the sherry, there were no lasting ill-effects. The incident certainly had its amusing aspects and caused me to recall another occasion when he had been a little devil!

Heather, Lisa and her school friend, Jonathan and I had travelled to London, where I was to sing during a major Spiritualist meeting at the Royal Albert Hall at which Gordon Higginson was demonstrating. At the close of the event we planned to travel overnight to catch the morning ferry to the Isle of Wight for a family holiday. As I rehearsed in the afternoon, all went well until we discovered that Jonathan had gone missing. We were all very worried because the Albert Hall is a huge warren of rooms and passageways on many storeys and we had absolutely no idea where to start looking for him. At long last he was discovered right at the very top of the building, in the highest possible corridor. We shouted to him again and again but he just would not come down. Eventually he did, but the next thing we knew, he had appeared in the royal box!

In the aftermath of the fire, the process of rebuilding our business had become the number one priority, consuming every bit of our time, energy and resources, and all else had to take second place. I had explained our predicament to the vendors of the house in Broughton Road and, to our relief, they kindly agreed not to sell the property to anyone else and to wait until we were once again in a position to go ahead with the purchase. They had already been let down by a previous prospective buyer, a pop star who had backed out at the last moment, and I believe they sensed that Heather and I would be true to our word and return to them as soon as we were able.

So it was that in March 1970, with the immediate trauma of the fire behind us, we visited the house once more and came to an agreement that we would go ahead with the purchase. We moved in on 1st May that year – a date, incidentally, which was declared auspicious by our friend Jose Benetto, then leader of the Essenes movement – and forty years later it is still my home.

* * * *

In 1971 I had the honour of meeting Lilian Bailey, one of the most renowned mediums of her day. Heather and I were introduced to her at a *Psychic News* dinner dance, held in London. We were very much aware of her reputation as a remarkable medium, so even a brief moment in her company was a privilege.

I am indebted to *Psychic News* and to my friend Roy Stemman for allowing me to use the following information which Roy included in his excellent book, *Spirit Communication.*

Lilian was in great demand by people from all walks of life but the incident to which I shall now refer was a closely guarded secret until after her passing and she never betrayed her oath of secrecy.

Out of the blue she received a request from a stranger to give a séance at a house in Kensington, London, to which she agreed. A limousine arrived to take her to a well-appointed property, from where she was taken to another address.

Lilian Bailey O.B.E.

Most unusually, she was required to put on a blindfold for the duration of the journey so that there would be no visual clues about the person or people she would be meeting. Again, she agreed.

Arriving at the second destination, she was eventually led into a room where she sensed others were gathered and she was asked to conduct the séance while still blindfolded. This was not a great hindrance to her since she often worked in a trance.

Puzzled, but nonetheless philosophical about the lengths to which people would go to test her mediumship, she drifted off into trance, allowing her main helper, Bill Wootton, and others in the next world, to speak through her lips.

After what seemed to her no time at all, she returned to normal consciousness and was told that she could now remove the blindfold.

As her eyes grew accustomed to the light, she surveyed the sitters. Sitting in a circle on gilt chairs were the Queen Mother, the Queen, Prince Philip, Princess Margaret, Princess Alexandra and the Duke of Kent.

This astonishing experience – which took place a year after the death of King George VI – had clearly been arranged in the hope of receiving a communication from the dead monarch. Given the calibre of Lilian Bailey's mediumship, it was almost certainly successful.

However, since she had been in a trance, the medium knew nothing of the conversation which had taken place between members of the British royal family and those from the spirit world who wished to speak to them.

Unsurprisingly, none of those who participated has ever commented directly on the secret séance.

Royal biographer and *Daily Telegraph* court correspondent, Ann Morrow, included this unique event in her book *The Queen Mother.*

She asked Gordon Adams, at that time an employee of *Psychic News*, if his mother-in-law Lilian Bailey had been unnerved when she removed the blindfold. He replied that his mother-in-law had had dealings with all sorts of people, such as the Chinese leader, Chiang Kai-Shek, and the King of Greece, so did not feel intimidated by royalty. It was almost like a day's work to her – her mediumship was so natural.

The Queen Mother is reported to have continued to phone Lilian for some time after that séance and further private sittings are said to have taken place. Eventually, when she came to terms with her loss and was clearly satisfied that the dead King continued to watch over her from the world of spirit, the Queen Mother asked the medium to come to Clarence House one last time.

Removing a piece of jewellery from the dress she was wearing, she pinned it on Lilian Bailey's shoulder saying, 'We don't own many personal posessions but I would like you to accept this.' No doubt the gift expressed her gratitude for the comfort she had received.

Almost immediately, she returned to public life.

Since the Royal family has never confirmed the story, can we be sure that this remarkable event actually took place?

Those who knew Lilian Bailey – who was awarded an O.B.E. for services in France during the First World War when she served with the Queen Mary's Army Auxiliary Corps – are adamant that she would not have invented such a story to boost her reputation.

She was already famous and, since the story was never published during her lifetime, it did not in any way affect her standing among Spiritualists or the public.

Helen Hughes and Lilian Bailey

More to the point is an observation by Ann Morrow. In writing her book, she received assistance from both the Queen Mother and her private secretary, Sir Martin Gilliat. They saw proofs of the book prior to its publication and raised no objection to inclusion of the report on the royal séance.

The story was repeated, again without objection, in Ann Morrow's *Without Equal: Her Majesty Queen Elizabeth the Queen Mother*, published in July 2000 to mark her centenary.

* * * *

Not long before I began work on this book I was in conversation with a friend who is a lay reader in a local Anglican church. Since he is devout in his belief and adherence to the teachings of Jesus I have a considerable degree of respect for him as a person, but having departed many years ago from my own acceptance of Christianity I obviously no longer share his views to the same extent.

Our chat turned to the subject of religion in general, and specifically to how people regard faiths different from their own. My friend then commented that Spiritualism is frowned upon and frequently spoken against by Christians. When I questioned him about the basis upon which he made this assertion he replied that there had never been authenticated comment on Spiritualism from the Christian community or its hierarchy. Hearing this, I asked him, 'Have you never read or become acquainted with the report on the 1937 investigation into Spiritualism by a committee of enquiry under the direction of the Archbishops of Canterbury and York?' He answered that he had not, and added that he doubted there had ever been such a thing.

Though I respected him, I could not help but be annoyed by his ill-informed statement, so I proceeded to tell him in no uncertain terms that there had indeed been such an investigation and that the seven investigators had written a report on behalf of the Church of England and its bishops which had been suppressed because it showed a majority in favour of Spiritualism by virtue of their enquiry into its many aspects.

What a shameful decision that suppression was, by so called honest, upright and true members of the House of Bishops – men who set themselves up as leaders of genuine morality.

However, the report was leaked anonymously to *Psychic News* and was duly published. Surely, I said to my friend, this suppression was against natural justice and would not be tolerated in today's world of openness. My friend was shocked and staggered for, as he commented, he had respect for me and knew I would not have made such a statement if it were not true. He was all the more staggered when I told him the names of the seven appointees to the Church of England committee of enquiry. I list them here, since I have no desire to shield them from you, my readers.

Dr Francis Underhill – Bishop of Bath and Wells

Dr W.R. Matthews – Dean of St Paul's Cathedral

Canon Harold Anson – Master of the Temple

Canon L.W. Grensted – Nolloth Professor of the Christian Religion at Oxford

Dr William Brown – Harley Street psychologist

Mr P.E. Sandlands, Q.C. – Barrister-at-Law

Lady Gwendolen Stephenson

From a personal point of view, I suppose this failure of the Anglican hierarchy to present the commission's true findings without fear or favour underlined my shame that at one time I had called myself an Anglican.

I still have many friends who are committed members of the Church of England; they are good-living, right-minded people, which is more than can be said for those archbishops who, after two years of research and investigation by their own appointees, chose to hush up their findings.

Following this discussion with my friend, I recalled an instance of similar ignorance which occurred in 1977.

My local paper, *The County Express*, had printed extracts from the parish magazine of Russells Hall Church in Dudley, in which the Revd James Butterworth warned against 'the terrible compulsion of Spiritualism and the occult' for people who were searching for something to believe in.

He continued by referring to 'the horrifying results of minds corroded with fear and with horror at themselves because they have been faced with Spiritualism.' Because I was a Spiritualist minister, *The County Express* gave me ample room to reply to these ill-informed comments, and in doing so I challenged Mr Butterworth to produce anyone who had become mentally deranged solely because of their involvement with Spiritualism. I described the vicar's reference to Spiritualism as being associated with witchcraft 'an ignorant insult'.

However, I did try to show him charity by stating that his mistake was perhaps due to ignorance of the subject matter – a situation which has inclined other bigots to make similar unfounded claims. I went on to say that if Mr Butterworth cared to undertake some research of his own he would find that I and other Spiritualists holding responsible positions had always condemned the Ouija board, and that the upsurge of interest in the paranormal did not necessarily equate with an upsurge of the occult.

I repeated my challenge to him to show me just one person who because of and only because of Spiritualism had become mentally deranged. I also pointed out to him that a recent survey had shown that, proportionately, clergymen were amongst the highest numbers of people seeking treatment for mental troubles.

Finally, I mentioned that Spiritualism's true purpose was to bring reassurance of life's continuity and reveal the universality of God, who, through the application of natural laws, extends his love to people of any race and religion, and indeed to those who have no religion at all.

The Revd Butterworth never replied.

Despite the lack of moral courage displayed by the Church of England's hierarchy in relation to Spiritualism, it is fair to record that a considerable number of well known Christians were quite open in their acknowledgement of the truths proclaimed by our movement. Prominent among them were the Rt Revd Dr Mervyn Stockwood, Anglican Bishop of Southwark; the Revd Dr Donald Soper, President of the Methodist Conference, who spoke at some large Spiritualist meetings; the American Episcopalian Bishop James Pike, who, incurring ridicule and censure from his fellow bishops, wrote extensively of his own experiences through the mediumship of Ena Twigg and others; and the

Revd G. Maurice Elliott, whose books re-interpreted a number of Biblical events, including the resurrection of Jesus, in the light of psychic phenomena, and Manfred Cassirer's 2003 book, *Miracles of the Bible*.

There was, however, one very positive spin-off which arose from the suppression of that Anglican report into Spiritualism. Under the guidance and determination of Colonel Reginald Lester, the Churches' Fellowship for Psychical and Spiritual Studies was brought into being. The Fellowship thrives to this day and has a large membership, including a good number of Christian clergy. It has as one of its patrons the most senior bishop in England today – the Revd and Rt Hon Richard Chartres, Bishop of London.

Chapter 7

Change and renewal

A unique club ✦ Significant changes for the SNU ✦ A song of unity ✦ Rededication of Stourbridge church ✦ Gordon Higginson ordains me as a minister

Once we were settled in Broughton Road and the business was again running smoothly, our house was ever open to the many mediums and speakers who served Stourbridge church – some quite famous, some quite remarkable. Over the years we also hosted at least four different television crews and various interviewers, and held church garden parties which were hugely popular.

Perhaps the most successful of these was attended by just short of a hundred people. Colourful awnings, stalls and games were laid out on the lawn, but no sooner had we got into the swing of things than the heavens opened and the rain came down in torrents. Everyone rushed into the house, the garage, the car port, but we were undeterred. No amount of rain was going to spoil our day.

Folk sat on the stairs, on the floor in the kitchen, in the conservatory – anywhere they could find a space. The entertainers we had booked even put on two separate shows so that people could change places to listen to them. We sang ourselves hoarse until the house vibrated. Yes, it was a good day!

Whoever we were entertaining, and whatever the occasion, my lovely wife never became flustered and made each and every person feel at home and welcome. As a result, my home is full of wonderful memories and unique experiences, but above all with a feeling of love.

* * * *

It was around this time that I was privileged to be invited to become a member of the Henkel Executive Club, which gave me, along with other members, the opportunity to visit some exceptional places which might otherwise have remained closed to us. All these trips were organised and paid for by Henkel, a large German company based on the outskirts of Frankfurt. Their factory complex is almost a town in itself, providing accommodation for their considerable workforce, along with a hospital, schools and and a wealth of other facilities. Henkel's factories produce a huge range of goods, including detergents and adhesives of every kind, some of which, such as Pritt and Solvite, we stocked in our warehouse.

Although Henkel club members were drawn from W.H. Smith, Boots, Menzies and other well-known high street outlets, I was often called upon to express thanks on behalf of us all when we we were taken on specially arranged mystery trips both in this country and abroad, and as will become apparent later in this book, on one memorable occasion I struggled rather hard to do so!

* * * *

At about the same time as I accepted Henkel's invitation to join the club, I also began to play a more active role in the national affairs of the SNU. As I recall the events of the 1970s, it has to be said that I do so with a degree of sadness, for many trials beset the organisation during those years.

I suppose the most pressing of these was the constant lack of sufficient funds with which to operate the Union and the Arthur Findlay College, for income invariably fell short of the relatively modest outgoings. The stresses and strains of dealing with this situation caused much anxiety, heated argument, and even the occasional falling out between those who were charged with the responsibility to oversee things and make decisions.

Perhaps I should not have been unduly surprised at this, since history shows that all religious organisations have their internal differences and problems, which too often culminate in the opposing factions splitting off and going their own way. To some extent this has also happened in the SNU. The Christian Spiritualist Society of Cardiff, the Corinthians, and also the Swansea church which the medium Stephen O'Brien now runs as an independent organisation, are but three examples among a number across the country. They serve to illustrate all too clearly that though we claim to be a spirit-guided movement we are also thoroughly human and should really learn to behave better.

Having said that, we should perhaps recognise how difficult the circumstances must have been for a SNU president and council made up of voluntary workers, with only a small number of paid employees, each in their own way contributing to legislating for several hundred churches which were allowed to operate as they chose, provided they complied with the broad outline of Spiritualism as stated in the Seven Principles.

Looking back, I also realise how complex was the task faced by the Union's area representatives who, in most cases, oversaw huge geographical areas. With the best will in the world it was almost impossible for one lone representative to keep in close contact with everything that was going on.

To some extent this was made easier when at a later date fourteen districts were created and the three-tier system was introduced to the Union. It provided for stages of devolution from the National Executive Committee to the council and then to the districts.

On this point, when the system was first proposed following a consultative conference and the setting up of a commission of enquiry, it was met with a considerable degree of hostility from some conference delegates who wanted to stick with the old ways.

Additional causes of concern at that time were the diverse systems of education within the SNU and the Lyceum. In an attempt to address the problems, the various individuals responsible in each body recommended that a joint SNU/SLU consulting committee be set up. I was invited to join this committee by its chairperson Olive Oscroft, and willingly accepted. My first experience of meeting with the other members was at Stansted Hall on 18th February 1977. Subsequent meetings were held at various locations and it would certainly be fair to say that progress was made on a matter which had hitherto given rise to much concern.

On the brighter side, the Union set up a number of propaganda meetings in large halls in different parts of the country with the two-fold purpose of promoting our message of life's continuity after physical death, and when possible, raising much needed funds. We had several gifted mediums and speakers who were not only capable of putting across our beliefs in a very effective way, but also had the power to galvanise and inspire large audiences. Prime among them were Ena Twigg, Gordon Higginson, William Redmond and Robin Stevens.

The friendships I formed during those years have left me with long-lasting memories and probably sustained me in my moments of doubt about the antics and behaviour of some members of the Union. Suffice it to say that, difficult though we found it at times, we came through that somewhat turbulent period and in the process gathered strength, along with a renewed determination to succeed.

* * * *

I have already alluded to the diverse groups which make up the Spiritualist movement. One such was the Greater World Christian Spiritualist League (now Association) which in 1975 invited me to sing some solo songs at a large public rally they were planning to hold in Birmingham Town Hall. It was a splendid event, which included an address by Scottish Spiritualist William Gardiner and a demonstration of clairvoyance by the well known medium, Gay Muir, and was attended by more than eight hundred people.

Whilst my allegiance to the SNU has always been beyond doubt, some members of the National Executive Committee and council nevertheless questioned how I could justify taking part in a major event hosted by another Spiritualist organisation. My answer to those critics was (and still is) that although the SNU and Greater World might differ in their views on the life and mission of Jesus, the two organisations certainly have more in common on the matter of survival after physical death than they have points which divide them.

Indeed, so important was this matter of a shared purpose that in 1974 I had been one of the SNU's representatives at joint meetings held between Greater World and the Union with the aim of building upon our common ground. The impetus for those meetings had come jointly from Gordon Higginson and Harry Smith, then president of Greater World, who had discussed the importance of placing a united face of Spiritualism before the general public. Sadly, the talks broke down after just a few meetings due to the inflexibility of some in both organisations. It was a significant disappointment, and today, as I write this book, there is still no prospect on the horizon of a united approach to Spiritualism.

It is worth noting here that, on being asked why Spiritualists had been denied any official representation, Sir Winston Churchill commented that we were 'a disorganised rabble'. In other words, the fragmented nature of our movement has been a significant stumbling block to the official acceptance and recognition we seek.

Considering that our common aim is to prove life after death, with all its implications, I was pleased at the time, and am still pleased today, to have had the honour of singing to a packed hall for the Greater World event. The message of survival is bigger by far than any one organisation.

* * * *

The summer of 1976 saw the culmination of almost two years of planning and hard work at Stourbridge church, as our second phase of extension and rebuilding reached its conclusion.

Although the church is now a bright and airy place, with modern, comfortable facilities, that was not always the case, and over my long years of association with it, it has experienced a great many ups and downs. When I first began to attend services, shortly after the Second World War, the facilities were very basic indeed, a far cry from what they are today.

For example, in those early days the only toilet facility was a very primitive brick cubicle on one side of the building, a relic from a bygone age which had to be emptied by nightsoil men on a regular basis. To say it was rudimentary would be something of an understatement – visiting it was not an experience for the delicate or faint-hearted!

In the church building itself we had only a small rostrum with a harmonium on one side, and on the other a small curtained-off area where the speaker would sit quietly prior to taking the service. In stark contrast to our present large social room, where refreshments are served after services, the only facility for making tea and coffee required a precipitous descent into the cellar by means of a flight of steps outside the building.

After the Second World War building materials were in very short supply, but eventually our plans for modernisation were passed by the local council and we secured the services of a builder and the necessary materials to construct a new entrance lobby with toilet facilities on either side, a small kitchen, an anteroom and a larger platform.

In spite of our limitations in those early days we held a number of social events including a rich-man, poor-man meal, through which we raised a good deal of money for African children. On another occasion we hosted a harvest supper with a good three-course meal for fifty-three people. Mind you, had the paying guests seen how we managed in that small kitchen, and in the makeshift extension, they may have raised their eyebrows, for we had been forced to build a temporary area made of handy angle covered with polythene, since the rain was pelting down and we needed to cover the calor gas grills on which we boiled the potatoes and peas in buckets. Thank goodness there were no health and safety regulations in those days, for if there had been, I fear our culinary efforts would have come to an untimely end!

Those drawbacks successfully overcome through our programme of rebuilding, church members, their families and friends, along with local dignitaries and many prominent members of the Spiritualist movement, gathered for a celebratory service of rededication conducted by Gordon Higginson.

Among our special guests was the legendary *Psychic News* editor Maurice Barbanell, who a few days later published an article about his visit to Stourbridge. I can do no better than to share his account of that special day, which appeared under the headline 'Mayor pays tribute at church's rededication.'

To attend last Saturday's rededication service at Stourbridge National Spiritualist Church, W. Midlands, following its extension, meant a round journey by car of 300 miles and took eleven hours, but it was a rewarding experience.

It was just over half a century earlier that local Spiritualists acquired what was then a gospel hall used by the Plymouth Brethren.

The date for this service had been postponed because Councillor Dennis Harty, Mayor of Dudley, wanted to be present with his wife, the lady mayoress.

The rededication was done by SNU president Gordon Higginson. He recalled that his first meeting in that church was over forty years ago, when he was fourteen. Gordon congratulated them on the magnificent transformation which doubles the church's accommodation.

'Spiritualism is not a branch of any other religion,' he stressed. Its profound message was, 'We are all gods in the making.'

The mayor unveiled a beautiful stained-glass window depicting the sun. It is the work of William Pardoe, a splendid craftsman, who presented it to the church.

The mayor thought it a fine thing these days for any church to increase its membership!

Church president Eric Hatton told the heart-warming, behind the scenes story leading to their accomplished task. Modestly, he said nothing about his own contribution, praising his enthusiastic, dedicated and hard-working committee and members as being responsible for it.

He, however, was the driving force for this new church when it was decided to rebuild on its site two years ago. One member told me, 'We would do anything for our president.'

Much of the strenuous work involved was of the do-it-yourself kind. As one example, Eric mentioned they had to move 1,200 tons of earth!

The money for the extension was raised by a variety of methods – coffee mornings, bring and buy sales, bazaars offering nearly new objects, with enough of these still stored for at least another dozen similar functions. Finally, an advance from the SNU building fund pool enabled the project to get under way.

Eric praised the local authority's co-operation. They agreed to construct a new road to the car park behind the church and made no charge for doing so, or for its maintenance.

He paid tribute to the local Unitarian church, whose minister was present, for accommodating them during the time when they could not meet.

Eric invited the oldest member of his church, James Foxall, whose 81st birthday was the previous Sunday, to address the audience. Then he asked someone even older, Percy Wilson, who is 83, to speak. Percy, looking a little frail, but very game, had come with his wife Winifred all the way from Oxford to be there.

Percy presented to the church its excellent amplification system. This provided opportunities, amongst other things, for recordings of classical music to be played.

In a firm voice, Percy said, 'I come to give you greetings from our pioneers.' He mentioned the fact, of which he was rightly proud, that he was dedicated to Spiritualism when only six weeks old. In the intervening period he had rededicated himself more than once!

When I, too, was asked to speak, I explained to the mayor and his wife the reason for the sunflower being chosen as a symbol in a badge many Spiritualists wear. It always turns its face to the sun.

I pointed out that it was not so very long ago that Spiritualists were 'rogues and vagabonds'. Our successful campaign to change antiquated laws, which denied us religious and legal freedom, had made us respectable, as shown by the presence of the mayor and mayoress. We still, however, had to reach the stage where we were respected.

Evidence of the splendid co-operation existing among the committee was the fact that a lavish tea was served, free of charge, to every one of the 200 people present. I pay tribute to these Midlands Spiritualists who are part of the backbone of our movement. They work unremittingly without thought of limelight or publicity. Throughout Britain their story can be duplicated many times.

My journey to Stourbridge took much longer than the one returning to London. I lost my way more than once. Even when Stourbridge was reached, I was misdirected. When I stopped to ask the way, my wife and I saw a genial middle-aged couple approaching. 'They look as if they are Spiritualists,' said my wife. She was right, and they were on their way to the church. So, by giving them a lift, we were able to arrive about fifteen minutes before the service began.

Percy Wilson   *Maurice Barbanell*

Clearly, Maurice Barbanell had enjoyed our special service of rededication, but he could not have enjoyed it any more than I did. It marked the fulfilment of a dream – not just my dream, but the dream of all the many church members who had worked with such commitment to make it a reality.

The joy and emotion I felt as each part of the service unfolded was difficult to put into words. For me, it had been an honour to be at the helm during such an exciting period of development, something that would have been beyond my wildest expectations when I first entered the church all those years before. Many compliments were paid by those who attended, and as Heather came to hug me afterwards and tell me how proud she was of me, my heart felt full to bursting.

* * * *

Less than six months later Stourbridge church was the setting for another milestone in my life as a Spiritualist, for after study and assessment I was invited to become a minister of the Spiritualists' National Union. It was a most significant step in my spiritual journey – a privilege which made me feel both honoured and humble, since the position calls for special qualities if one is to carry out and live true to its obligations.

Being a minister of the SNU puts one on equal terms with ministers of other religions, enabling one to carry out the same duties as they do. Funerals, weddings and naming ceremonies, hospital visiting and the signing of passports and other official forms are just some of the many tasks we fulfil. We are often called upon to provide a listening ear for anyone who is going through troubled times, or simply needs to talk, and we will also visit Spiritualists in prison, if asked.

The service took place on 2nd April and was conducted by Gordon Higginson, who was by then president of the Union. It was extremely moving and never to be forgotten – an emotional event not only for me, but also for my family and the many friends and colleagues who were present.

Every candidate for ordination must have a sponsor, and mine was Albert Taylor, with whom I had been friends since he first came to visit me in the RAF hospital back in the 1940s. At the grand old age of 90 he was by then the movement's oldest minister, and a medium who had given more than 60 years' loyal service.

My sister Laura wrote a special hymn for me, just as she had done for Heather and me on our wedding day. It began with the words:

King of the sun and sea,
Thy servant seeks to honour thee.
All that he has to give,
He offers with humility.

At the close of the service I was greatly surprised and touched to be presented with an antique solid silver salver on behalf of the church.

Whilst Spiritualist ministership does not confine itself to one particular church, I have always seen my role as being that of pastoral care for our community there. I can only say that in showing care and expressing feeling for that community I have received an abundance of love in return.

* * * *

There has been much discussion and debate about whether we have an allotted time on earth and our passing is almost predetermined, or whether we ourselves can influence our time of departure. Having heard and read many unusual experiences people have recounted, I still find it difficult to pronounce categorically on one side or the other of the argument.

Just after her eightieth birthday, Sally Ferguson, a wonderful medium and great friend to whom I have referred elsewhere in this book, sustained terrible injuries while travelling as a passenger in a car which crashed. Suffering from a broken spine, she was rushed to Birmingham Accident Hospital in Bath Row. Her injuries were devastating and doctors did not expect her to live for more than a few days.

As soon as we heard of the accident, Heather and I went straight to visit Sally, who told us with firm conviction that she would not die until our daughter, Lisa, had reached her twenty-first birthday, which was on 17th December. Sally loved Lisa and had watched her grow and blossom into a lovely young woman. She was therefore determined to remain in this world until Lisa had reached such an important milestone.

Thereafter, we visited Sally daily, and on a number of occasions were jolted by the shrill ringing of alarm bells attached to various pieces of equipment, thinking that they must signify Sally's imminent passing. Such was her determination, though, that she always managed to overcome these crises.

When we visited Sally the evening before Lisa's birthday, we were amazed to find her very cheerful. The next day, Heather and I were called urgently to the hospital and, on arrival, found a very different Sally from the one we had seen less than twenty-four hours before.

Sally Ferguson

Visibly weaker, she held our hands and whispered reassuringly, 'Don't worry, I'm all right. They are here to collect me.' With that, she closed her eyes and was gone. A nursing sister ushered us gently away and drew the curtains around the bed. Both she and another nurse burst into tears.

As the sister composed herself, she told us that on the day before, the nurses had been carrying out various procedures for Sally when a man appeared in the ward. He was unknown to the nursing staff and the sister told him in no uncertain terms that he should leave. Hearing this, Sally said calmly, 'Don't worry, it's only Bert. He's counting the buttons, but I've told him he's got to wait a bit longer. I'm not ready yet.' When the sister and nurse looked up, the man was gone.

Heather and I were intrigued by this account and asked the sister what the man had looked like. As she described him, we knew for certain that it had been Bert Ferguson, for Sally had given us a photograph of him some years before. They had been a devoted couple, and in his eagerness to take his wife to her new home, he had arrived just a little early.

Chapter 8

Harry Edwards

Just a few months before my ordination, news of the passing of the great healer Harry Edwards had deeply saddened the Spiritualist community. I had known Harry for almost thirty years and shared a platform with him on many occasions. As I look back over the impressive healings I was privileged to witness through his outstanding gift, I am ever grateful to have seen such wonders with my own eyes.

Each of us has many experiences in life. Some are taken for granted and soon forgotten, while others stand out, not only for the impact they make on us at the time, but because they remain as treasured memories of events which are almost unique and unlikely ever to be repeated.

There have been a number of outstanding individuals who were blessed with the gift of healing, but none was as dedicated and remarkable as my friend Harry Edwards, whom, as I have already said, I first met in 1947, when he gave me spiritual healing at his recently opened centre in Burrows Lea, Surrey.

In spite of his considerable fame, Harry was by nature a very humble man, and remained so to the end of his earthly days. His desire at all times was to use his healing power to help people, no matter what their station. He treated folk from all walks of life – rich or poor, it made no difference to him. Royalty benefited from his marvellous gift, as did medical doctors. He was equally respected by serious and unbiased researchers, a number of whom studied his work in detail. Whoever he treated and healed, it was almost without exception to their benefit.

Harry had few spare moments in such a busy life, for his extraordinary abilities were in constant demand. But for each of us there must be some moments of relaxation, and Harry loved to spend those times painting and reading the detective stories he so much enjoyed.

In his public demonstrations, which usually took place in very large halls, he often astonished the assembled crowds by showing that painfully obvious physical deformity could be treated in a matter of minutes, and a visible transformation be brought about. There was no massage or manipulation of the kind which some complementary practitioners use with varying degrees of success, but there, before our very eyes, the lame were able to walk, the blind able to see, and the severely crippled were enabled to do moderate exercise. It defied belief, except that it happened, and all without pain to the individual being treated.

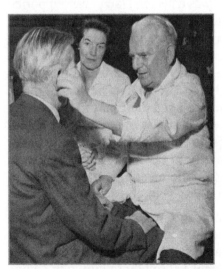

Harry Edwards healing deafness in the Sanctuary at Burrows Lea (Mrs Olive Burton in the background)

Harry used no ostentatious prayers, nor was there a requirement to believe in any form of religion, including Spiritualism. No pious attitude was demanded or expected. There was simply an indefinable 'something' in the atmosphere which enabled some remarkable cures to be achieved through the touch of his healing energy.

During his many years of ministry to

Harry Edwards studies requests for healing with
colleagues Ray and Joan Branch

those who were in need, both as an ordained Spiritualist minister and more especially as a healer, Harry was supported by Olive and George Burton and Ray and Joan Branch. Indeed, Ray and Joan were associated with Harry's healing centre at Burrows Lea for a period of some forty years, from 1962 until 2002, continuing Harry's work after his passing in 1976. They were extremely fond of him, as he was of them. Harry's family members also played their part in supporting his work, helping to deal with the mass of requests for absent healing which came by post to Burrows Lea on a daily basis. Though they remained quietly in the background and were never seen on stage at his public meetings, their loyalty to him and his healing mission was very considerable.

I recall one particular occasion when Harry was giving a public demonstration of healing in front of a large crowd at the Civic Hall in Wolverhampton. A lady who was a member of our church in Stourbridge was brought to him with a huge goitre under her chin. To be honest, it was so enormous that she actually looked quite a mess. The lady and her husband were quite comfortably off and had visited numerous doctors in the hope of a cure, always being advised that an operation would be too dangerous to undertake.

Calmly, in full view of the large audience, Harry placed one hand on the goitre and the other on the lady's neck area, talking to her all the while. I was sitting close by and had a very clear view of what was happening. There, before our very eyes, the goitre began to diminish in size, and as Harry finally took his hand away, we saw that it had reduced to almost nothing. It was so amazing – a wonderful incident that could never be forgotten. For months afterwards, people in our church were questioning whether the goitre would return, but five years later there was not the slightest sign of it.

Amongst many other wonderful cures, I witnessed one in the 1960s which touched me so deeply that it brought tears to my eyes. Harry was demonstrating healing in a large public venue and a small boy was brought to him, so badly deformed that his twisted and misshapen body could barely support itself in his mother's lap. Yet within a few minutes of healing, and without any physical manipulation, the little boy's deformity had disappeared, and in full view of the crowd he was able to stand unaided for the first time in his life.

The look of bewilderment on the child's face, coupled with his mother's outburst of tearful joy and gratitude, was without doubt the most moving thing I have ever witnessed. I was not alone in that reaction – many others who witnessed this healing (dare I call it a miracle?) were similarly brought to tears. So moving was it for me that, even as I write about it decades later, goose pimples are on my arms and emotion blurs my vision.

Apart from the many healing cures of human beings that were attributed to his name, Harry was also called upon to treat animals, and did so with considerable success.

In the 1960s he took part in a series of programmes broadcast by the BBC, in which he was very closely questioned by a sceptical British Medical Association. The principal questioner was a man who was obviously hostile toward the possibility of spiritual healing, and conducted himself in a manner to which Spiritualists took exception. Harry, on the other hand, was most calm and collected throughout the three programmes, always emphasising that spiritual healing was a force beyond anything which medical science had yet come to recognise. He took no personal credit for any treatments or cures achieved through his healing mediumship, stressing that it was not he who was responsible for healing, but an energy which flowed through him. He was assisted in this by two helpers from the world of spirit – the scientists Louis Pasteur and Joseph Lister.

Hostile though those programmes were, they probably helped to form a bridge between the medical profession and spiritual healing. There was no sudden or dramatic breakthrough, but in subsequent years, and by virtue of Harry's work with the NFSH, healers were allowed little by little into hospitals – something which has now become relatively commonplace.

After Harry's years of dedicated work in the field of healing the sick, the National Federation of Spiritual Healers, of which he was president, decided to organise a special

Five thousand people filled the Royal Albert Hall to celebrate Harry Edwards' 80th birthday

meeting at London's Royal Albert Hall, where tributes would be paid to him, and he would give a demonstration of spiritual healing.

The event was to coincide with Harry's eightieth birthday and many famous people expressed a wish to be present, for a lot of them had benefited from his extraordinary ability. Numerous luminaries of the Spiritualist movement were present, including *Psychic News* editor Maurice Barbanell and Percy Wilson, and I clearly remember that Gordon Higginson gave an impressive demonstration of mediumship. The hall was absolutely packed out.

I was greatly honoured to be invited to sing some solos in tribute to Harry, one of which he requested personally. It was entitled *'If I can help somebody as I pass along'* – a most appropriate song for a man who had spent his life helping others.

Today, as I reflect back on that occasion, and recall my feelings of nervousness as I stood up to sing to the crowds in that enormous building, I remember the relief and sense of satisfaction I felt as I sang my final notes, which were greeted with considerable applause. I can hardly believe that it was I who sang to that audience of five thousand people! My family were present and were very proud. So was I.

Chapter 9

Comfort and joy

A speedy spirit return ✦ *Dancing the night away* ✦ *A remarkable spirit portrait* ✦ *A trio of surprises* ✦ *Wedding fever* ✦ *I take to the streets* ✦ *A new joy in our lives*

Throughout our business life, Heather, Lisa, Jon and I always endeavoured to show understanding to the staff we employed, creating a caring family atmosphere. One example of this was when Ena, a most dedicated member of staff who had worked for us for almost fifteen years, asked for time off to look after her mother, Mrs Jepson, who was seriously ill and not expected to live much longer.

On Friday evening, after Ena had been away for five days, Heather and I decided that we should visit her to offer any help which might be needed. On arrival we found that both Ena and her sister looked very tired. They also confided to us that they were fearful of staying up all night with a dying person. I therefore offered to come back and sit with their mother through the night once I had taken Heather home.

When I returned, the two sisters went to the next room to try to get some much-needed sleep. I went into their mother's room to sit beside her and watch her breathing. During the hours which followed I brushed her lovely silver hair back from her face, then with a small ball of cotton wool dipped in water I moistened her dry lips. With another moistened cotton wool ball I gently wiped her brow.

She survived through the night and I went home to sleep for a little while. After lunch, Heather and I returned to Ena's home, only to find that Mrs Jepson had passed away at nine that morning and the undertakers had removed her body to their chapel of rest.

Leaving the house a while later, we made our way straight to London, where I was due to give a couple of addresses at the Spiritual Mission in Pembridge Place. The demonstrator was to be the Scottish medium Albert Best.

As he began his demonstration on Sunday morning, he gave detailed evidence to various members of the congregation. After a while he said that he was conscious of someone who had not as yet been buried and in fact had only passed away a matter of hours before. Could anyone accept this communicator? he asked.

No one spoke up in response to his question, but then Albert turned to me on the platform and said, 'I'm told that you know this lady who passed. Is this so?' I answered that it was. He then proceeded to describe in detail the tasks I had performed for her the previous night. I was staggered by the accuracy and precision of this communication, which Albert then amplified by giving further personal details.

It is worth noting that neither Mrs Jepson nor her daughters were Spiritualists, which goes to show that you do not have to be one in order to communicate from the Higher Life or indeed to receive mediumistic evidence of life after death.

* * * *

Over the years, Stourbridge weeks and J.V. Trust weeks have been held at Stansted Hall during the summer months. Since I usually played a prominent part in them I always tried to ensure that, aside from the learning aspects of the events, a true atmosphere of friendship and happiness flourished.

Some of those weeks were held around the time of the Summer solstice, and from time to time I persuaded people to join me at about ten o'clock at night for something a little out of the ordinary. We would gather around the tulip tree in the peaceful grounds where, to the accompaniment of music, we sang, linked hands and swayed gently in time with the melodies. We also recalled and paid tribute to Spiritualist pioneers, loved ones, friends and helpers on the other side of life.

Many who were present have told me that during this shared activity they experienced a sense of unity the like of which they had never known before. Suffice it to say that at the conclusion of the event, all of us were left with a feeling of upliftment and joy as we shared in an atmosphere that was unprecedented.

As a footnote to this story, some invitees on a J.V. Trust week had never experienced this marking of the solstice, and I mentioned to them almost jokingly that maybe we could try it. But as the day wore on and the evening light began to fade, I felt a little tired and decided to go to bed, forgetting what I had suggested. I must have dozed off to sleep when a loud knock came on the bedroom door. Hugh Davis and another person were there, telling me that a host of people were on the front lawn of the college waiting for me to lead them in the solstice experience! I was truly embarrassed, for it had slipped my mind completely.

I hurriedly swapped my pyjamas for a shirt and trousers and proceeded to the gardens with my two minders, to be greeted by loud cheers from the assembled group. Where I got the inspiration and energy from I shall never know, but one thing was for sure – it was a great success and would remain as a treasured memory, not only for me but for all who were present.

* * * *

One day in 1980, during another Stourbridge week at Stansted Hall, I was confined to bed with a bout of dizziness. The respected psychic artist Coral Polge was visiting the Hall and was due to give a talk about her gift, along with a demonstration of her inspired drawings of people who had passed from this life. I greatly regretted that I was unable to be present, but I was later informed by those who were, that with the exception of one particular drawing, each of the portraits was accepted as being an image of someone's loved one. There was one portrait which no one could recognise, and that seemed strange considering that all the others had been so readily accepted.

Heather, who had attended the demonstration, was asked if she would show this portrait to me when I was feeling better, to see if I could recognise the person Coral had drawn. Certain references had been made to me during the demonstration and it was thought that the drawing might perhaps have some meaning to me.

The day before Coral's demonstration I had spoken about a funeral service I had conducted in Redditch. It had been for Andrew Weston, a young man aged just seventeen who had been killed while out riding his motorcycle. I mentioned that I had not known him personally, nor had I met any of his family until his mother came to Stourbridge asking that I take his funeral service.

I well recall that she requested a particular song – 'Kum Ba Yah', which contains the verse 'Someone's crying Lord, Kum Ba Yah'. I was intrigued by this and asked her why she had chosen it. She explained that her boy had been a good lad – not a tearaway – and that as he had driven round a bend, a coach carrying thirty-eight school children had come hurtling towards him on the wrong side of the road. Had he not swerved to avoid it and therefore hit a wall and been killed, thirty-eight mothers might have been 'crying Lord', she said.

Having never met Andrew Weston or seen a photograph of him, when I saw Coral's portrait it meant nothing to me. Nor did the name 'Fred' – which had apparently been given in connection with the drawing – carry any significance for me. However, when I returned home I got in touch with Mr and Mrs Weston and they came to visit me some days later. No sooner had they seen the portrait than they shouted out, 'That's our Andrew!' They then pulled out a bag of photographs of Andrew which left no doubt that the likeness was so close as to be unmistakable.

After a few minutes I told them of the manner in which the portrait had come about – but I added that the name of Fred meant nothing to me. At this, Mrs Weston told me excitedly that Andrew's dad had called him Fred.

Most interestingly, Coral had not arrived at Stansted by the time I spoke of the hundred bikers and other people who had attended the funeral service, and as I have said, I was not present when she had sensed and drawn Andrew Weston. The ways of communication are many and varied, and I will never cease to be impressed by the ingenuity of those who wish to contact us after they have so-called 'died'.

Left to right: Heather, Gordon Higginson, Coral Polge and myself in our home

* * * *

During 1981, three unexpected events occurred in my life within the space of just a few months. The first of these was an invitation to be interviewed on radio by Chris Tarrant, who, though very well known now, was at that time an up-and-coming research journalist for BBC Birmingham. He had been informed about my long association with psychical research and the people I had encountered during my investigations.

His questioning was at times very sharp, probing the events which had shaped my beliefs. There were moments when I felt somewhat unhappy with those questions, perhaps because they were so direct and gave some impression of hostility, but by the end of the interview I had formed the opinion that Chris was reasonably fair-minded. As I reflect back upon what took place, I am disposed to think he was probably more sympathetic to Spiritualism and psychical research than most journalists.

The broadcast was a live one, which I guess would be daunting for some people, but I had not been unduly concerned about it. It was only when I returned to my office later that Heather and my staff commented on the fact that I had had no rehearsal or preparation for the programme. 'Why on earth did you do it?' they asked. My reply was that if we Spiritualists didn't take every opportunity to put our case forward, be it by radio or TV, we would never convince people of the genuineness of what had been revealed to us. That response might seem a trifle bombastic on my part, as might having done the programme without rehearsal or much preparation, but I keep in mind the words of the old hymn: 'Dare to be a Daniel; dare to stand alone'.

A short while after the Chris Tarrant interview Heather, our church member Cissie Shaw and I were once again at Stansted Hall, organising a Stourbridge week on which one of our tutors was Mavis Pittilla. All three ladies were intrigued when I told them out of the blue that I had been asked by Henkel to make my way to Hatfield airport, in Hertfordshire. The fact was that I had been notified of this event two weeks or so earlier, but a number of other important things had occupied my time in the intervening period, and I had temporarily forgotten the date until, all of a sudden, I received a phone call at Stansted reminding me that I was expected at Hatfield airport the next day.

I arrived there to find a number of the executive club members already assembled, and shortly afterwards we were ushered onto a twin-engined plane without a word about where we were headed, in the mysterious cloak-and-dagger style so typical of the Henkel 'minders'.

Much of the flight was in fairly thick mist and it was only after one-and-a-half hours that we finally caught a glimpse of mountains far below us. Speculation was rife amongst us as we tried to guess our ultimate destination. Some club members suggested we were over Norway, then a couple of 'wags' shouted down the plane: 'Come on Eric! With your psychic ability you should be able to tell us where we're going!' Needless to say I did not rise to the bait, and simply said that we were all in for a surprise. A few minutes later our speculation came to an end as the plane descended onto the runway of a small airport which turned out to be Wick, in the north of Scotland. But why Wick? we wondered, for it seemed somewhat remote from civilisation and we couldn't work out what Henkel might be planning in such an out-of-the-way location.

Our questions mounted as we got off the plane and were invited to board a rather rickety old coach. As I settled in my seat and prepared for the next leg of this strange mystery journey, it crossed my mind that we might perhaps be going to visit an isolated Scottish distillery. This guess was soon proved wrong, for after a short journey we found ourselves in front of an imposing and rugged-looking building which we quickly discovered was the Castle of Mey, a favourite retreat of the Queen Mother, some six miles west of John O'Groats.

No sooner had we crossed the threshold than a sizeable glass of whisky was handed to each of us. Although I was not much of a whisky drinker, we were given no opportunity to refuse it, so I did the decent thing and drank it down as expected. Then, in an atmosphere of merriment, yet with great respect for our surroundings, we set off on a conducted tour around most of the castle, with its stunning views across the Pentland Firth to the Orkney Islands.

Lunch followed, and was a grand affair, with a traditional kilted piper playing as we enjoyed the excellent food and

The Castle of Mey

wines served to us in the regal surroundings of the castle's dining room.

Speaking of wine, I shall ever be grateful that I rationed myself in that department, for even so, my legs started to buckle when I was asked to give a vote of thanks to our hosts, and I had to steady myself by holding on to the huge banqueting table before me. Even to my own ears, my words seemed to emerge a little jumbled, but I drew comfort from the fact that my fellow diners were somewhat more 'tippled' than I was and probably didn't notice!

As we flew back to Hatfield I tried to work out how Henkel had managed to secure the invitation to such an exclusive place, it being carefully guarded for the royalty it belonged to. I can only think they must have had very persuasive ways.

Arriving back at Stansted I found my fellow tutors gathered in the lounge and began excitedly to tell them about the escapade I had just enjoyed. They found it hard to believe until I showed them the cut glass souvenir of the Castle of Mey and then allowed them a 'wee dram' of the special whisky I had been given. Suffice to say, after tasting it they were convinced!

The third in my series of unexpected events took place shortly after that memorable day at Mey.

I had occasion to visit the Spiritualist church in Hinckley, Leicestershire, where at that time there was an excellent minister named Marjorie Hathaway. She was very friendly with the famous comedian Larry Grayson, who hosted his own popular TV show, and she introduced me to him, explaining that he often visited the church.

He was kind and very friendly towards me, admitting that he had a strong belief in life after death, having received much convincing evidence of survival. Prior to our meeting I had not been an ardent fan of Larry's, but the content of our brief conversation was well worth remembering. The sometimes silly style of his TV shows was in sharp contrast to his intelligent grasp of spiritual matters. How wrong we can be in our impressions about a person of whom we know little.

* * * *

Even as I had visited the Queen Mother's Scottish retreat, the royal family had been at the forefront of everyone's mind with the announcement that the Prince of Wales and Lady Diana Spencer were to marry. Speculation about a possible engagement had been rife for months, and across Britain, and indeed the rest of the world, there was great excitement. Commemorative items rattled off the production lines to meet the demands of people clamouring for a memento of the unique occasion.

Gordon Higginson and I felt that it would be fitting to reflect the good wishes of Spiritualists by making some tangible gift to the royal couple, and began to give some thought to an appropriate item.

The town of Stourbridge has long been famous for its glass making, and I decided to approach a small firm of cut glass specialists based near to our own business premises. The principal designer and fine glass cutter responded enthusiastically when I asked if he could cut the image of Stansted Hall onto a large bowl. After seeing photographs of the Hall, he told me, 'Well, I'm doing something special for two famous and high-ranking people but yours shall be even better than theirs!' I never saw their finished bowl but ours was certainly a superb piece of work.

Not long after collecting it, Gordon, Heather and I travelled to London and delivered the engraved bowl to Buckingham Palace. Before handing it over, we had taken a number of pictures of it, but they did not really do justice either to the bowl itself or to the engraving of Stansted Hall.

Nonetheless, they form an important and interesting record for future generations of Spiritualists.

A short time after the royal wedding had taken place in July that same year, I received a letter from the prince's equerry, conveying the thanks of the royal couple and adding that our gift had given them great pleasure. A copy of this letter is on display at Stansted Hall.

The engraved bowl sent to Charles and Diana for their wedding

There is an interesting and rather touching sequel to this story. Several months later, Prince Charles was carrying out an official engagement, in the course of which he was meeting with a group of older people in a parade. Pausing to speak with one gentleman, the prince noticed that he was wearing a badge on his lapel.

'That's a badge I've not seen before,' he said. 'What is it?'

'It's a Spiritualist badge, Sir,' came the reply.

At this, Prince Charles responded, 'My wife and I have a beautiful bowl given to us by Spiritualists as a wedding present, and it has brought us great pleasure.'

When you consider the hundreds, if not thousands of wedding gifts the couple had received, it is impressive to say the least that the prince had such immediate recall of the one we had given.

* * * *

Music was on the agenda again as I set off for the University of Lampeter, in Cardiganshire. This time, however, I was not going to sing, but to take part in a weekend seminar which Heather and I had been invited to attend.

During a very happy and rewarding few days we shared the company of some good lecturers, including one of the funniest men I have ever met. Leslie Hitchins was a Spiritualist minister from Manchester, and had a seemingly inexhaustible repertoire of humorous stories which amply demonstrated that you don't always have to be poker-faced to be a good minister!

Another lecturer was Professor Ian Parrott, a musicologist highly respected in his field. Ian had devoted huge amounts of his time to studying the very remarkable inspired musical compositions of Rosemary Brown, who had become well known for the complex works she channelled from great composers in spirit.

Ian was able to convey vividly to us what an extraordinary lady she was, for she had never studied music in any formal way, or learnt to play the piano, yet he and other musical authorities had been overwhelmed by the quality of the compositions they had heard and examined.

* * * *

In company with three other people, I undertook to pound the pavements and carry out market research on behalf of the SNU, both among its own members and with the general public. This was a new step for us, one I felt was important since it might provide us with some up-to-date information on how Spiritualists were viewed by wider society, and reveal whether or not they considered Spiritualism a religion in its own right.

As I had expected, I was given a mixed reception on the streets and my findings were extremely varied. One thing stood out more sharply than any other: many people did not know that we Spiritualists hold a passionate belief in God. In response to this I pointed out politely and calmly that long-ingrained views among the Christian churches concerning Spiritualism were frequently based upon a fallacy. Though we may not see the life of Jesus as they do, we believe strongly in the power of prayer and its accompanying all-embracing reverence for God, which were surely integral parts of Jesus' life. Hearing these points, people's attitudes towards me seemed to shift noticeably and I was accorded some respect.

* * * *

On the home front, excitement was at full throttle as we awaited the imminent birth of our first grandchild. Lisa's pregnancy had progressed perfectly normally and she was fit and well, but like all prospective grandparents we were anxious that the birth should be a routine matter with no complications.

A week or so before the baby was due, Lisa and Heather were out strawberry picking at a nearby farm, when Lisa confided that she was experiencing contractions. Heather was concerned and wanted to take Lisa straight to the hospital, but Lisa was determined to finish the task at hand before she went. Our beautiful grandson Tristan was born during the early evening of 11th May at the Wordsley Hospital. The birth had proceeded exactly as it should, and mother and baby were doing fine. Heather and I were absolutely over the moon in our elation at becoming grandparents.

Chapter 10

On our travels

A new role in the SNU ✦ A white-knuckle ride ✦ The Bank at Monte Carlo ✦ A cherished private visit ✦ TV cameras come to Stourbridge

By 1985 I had been active in the SNU for more than thirty years and felt privileged when, at that year's annual general meeting, it was announced that the membership had elected me to serve as Gordon Higginson's vice-president. Gordon and I were great friends and shared many of the same aspirations for the Union, so I relished the opportunity of serving alongside such a dynamic and gifted president.

I continued to address large public meetings and to chair demonstrations for some of our well-known mediums. One such occasion in the mid 1980s was for Doris Fisher Stokes who, in the early years of her work as a medium, had visited the church in Stourbridge on a number of occasions. In those days she was known as plain Doris Stokes, only adding the Fisher when she started to become famous. There is no doubt in my mind that her mediumship was better in those early days than it was when she was later appearing in the great public halls, and this particular occasion served to underline that view.

A half-day seminar was to be held in the Malvern Theatre, Worcestershire. and I was to chair a meeting at which Doris and Gordon Higginson would demonstrate. It had been decided that Doris should work first, so I welcomed the large audience, introduced her, and the demonstration got under way.

After a while it became clear to me that Doris, who was by that time extremely well known, was struggling a bit. Going to a recipient, she announced, 'I've got a Mary here.' This information was met with a blank look, and the recipient told Doris, 'No, it isn't Mary.'

'Well, is it Marion? Yes, that's it!' Doris persisted.

'No, it's Margaret,' offered the recipient helpfully.

'Oh, is it Margaret?' asked Doris.

Well, Doris had done this a few times and I felt her demonstration wasn't flowing too well. A short while later I decided that she was doing no one any favours, particularly herself, so I said to her quietly, 'Right Doris, you can conclude now – your time's up,' though in truth it wasn't.

But she challenged me, saying, 'Oh no. I've got more.'

'I'm sure you have,' I said to her, 'but I feel we should move on.'

Though she did not show it overtly, I could sense her almost violent mental reaction to me. She was not at all pleased. Nevertheless, she sat down and Gordon took over. His demonstration was totally different, giving very accurate and detailed information.

At the end of the meeting, Doris came to me straight away and reprimanded me in no uncertain terms.

'You shouldn't have pulled me up!' she said angrily. 'I had more things to give.'

She was very much taken aback that anybody would have the audacity to stop her in her tracks!

* * * *

At about the same time as I was elected vice-president I had also become chairman of Key Consortium, an organisation which still exists today, though it is now known as Impact. The idea behind it was that wholesale stationers from all parts of Britain and Ireland would work together, primarily to get good prices, but also to bring out their own promotions.

Initially the consortium had been an amalgam of just five or six firms, of which I became the secretary, but gradually others came in and it grew steadily. We soon had members in Northern Ireland, Eire, Scotland and places all over England. By the time I was elected chairman the consortium encompassed some twenty-four companies, and at times I found it all a bit too much to handle.

A much needed opportunity for relaxation came in the form of a Henkel Club trip to the beautiful alpine resort of St Moritz, and what an experience it was! It was wintertime, and the sight of the beautiful snow-capped mountains was one I shall never forget.

Henkel had made arrangements for us to go up into those mountains for an experience with a difference. They had negotiated with a bobsleigh company which ran special events and competitions, so that we ourselves could have the opportunity to take a high-speed ride down the mountain.

It was a perfect winter's day – the sun was shining, the snow was crisp and we were all excited, if a bit apprehensive. A friend of mine, Peter, took a look at me and said, 'Come on Eric, we'll go together.' So, knees knocking, I got into the bobsleigh behind the pilot. Peter sat behind me, and behind Peter was the all-important brake man. We were in the hands of both of them, the pilot and the brake man, and I confess that the adrenalin was beginning to course through me.

Still, it was all very exciting, and we watched some army lads go down the first part of the run, pick up speed and disappear out of sight. Then it was our turn. I hadn't realised, although I should have done, how the bobsleigh would twist and turn at exceedingly high speeds. We had hard helmets on but I was quite concerned.

My head was down, my knuckles white, and I thought to myself, 'Good God – if we hit a wall we'll be over the top and that'll be it!' It seemed as if we swung from side to side, at the same time gathering huge speed. I'd looked forward to the ride, but boy was I glad when we got to the bottom! I have a framed certificate, shown opposite, dated 5th February

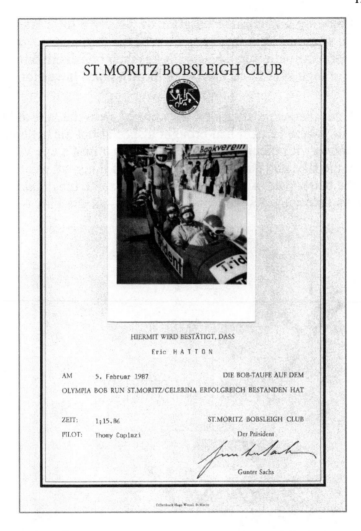

ST.MORITZ BOBSLEIGH CLUB

HIERMIT WIRD BESTÄTIGT, DASS

Eric H A T T O N

AM   5. Februar 1987   DIE BOB-TAUFE AUF DEM

OLYMPIA BOB RUN ST.MORITZ/CELERINA ERFOLGREICH BESTANDEN HAT

ZEIT: 1;15.86   ST.MORITZ BOBSLEIGH CLUB

PILOT: Thomy Caplazi   Der Präsident

                                Gunter Sachs

Offsetdruck Hugo Wetzel, St.Moritz

1987, which, strangely, makes no mention of the bobsleigh's stomach-churning speed of up to 94 miles per hour.

We clambered out of the bobsleigh (with much relief) and it was transferred to a special steel-lined lorry. We climbed in after it, taking seats on either side. Suffice it to say that our journey back up the mountain was considerably less nail-biting than our journey down. On arrival at the top, the first place I called at was the toilet!

Enjoying a much-needed glass of whisky a little later, I heard of an incident that had occurred the day before, when two British soldiers had been killed as their bobsleigh turned over at high speed and they were thrown out. I never forgot it.

Later that same afternoon we were taken to the lake at St Moritz where Henkel had brought a special hot air balloon, complete with picnic hampers, to give us a bird's eye view over the lake and part of St Moritz itself. I think we went up to the better part of 700 feet and we saw some breathtaking views below us. As we came back down, all the kids were

coming out of school. One in particular was desperate to have a go, so I put him in the basket with me and up I went again. I was sixty years old and I thought twice was enough at my age. It had been quite a day one way and another!

A year later the Henkel Club embarked on yet another secret journey, and it was only as the plane circled over Nice prior to landing that we began to get a hint of what might be in store for us. Emerging from the airport we were transported by luxurious coach into the bustling and brightly-illuminated city of Monte Carlo and thence to one of the best hotels in the principality. This alone would have left us with a lasting and wonderful memory, but as events unfolded we began to see that no expense had been spared in arranging our trip.

After settling in to the glorious surroundings of the hotel, we were escorted to the dining room where a superb meal was served to us. An orchestra played as we dined, and as we absorbed the wonderful, happy atmosphere and enjoyed the excellent food, we were more than a little intrigued to know what the next surprise might be.

Dinner over, we were escorted by expert guides, as well as the Henkel contingent, into the streets of Monte Carlo. They were alive with activity as residents and visitors alike moved towards a huge marquee, which was in the midst of a number of elegant stalls selling food, drinks and other delights. People danced with festive excitement in the surrounding area.

We were then told that the exclusive and world-renowned Monte Carlo Circus was to be our next eye-opener. Top artists and the very best acts from around the world were to compete for a prestigious and sought-after title.

The most luxurious seats were occupied by dignitaries from many countries, including royalty and ambassadors, and we were delighted to discover that our seats were amongst the best. Suddenly, just before the show was about to commence, the audience rose from their seats and the musicians began to play Monaco's National Anthem. Who should walk to the vacant seats two or three rows in front of ours but Prince Rainier, Prince Albert, Princess Caroline and other members of their family. What a privilege it was for us, and most certainly for me. The circus acts were superb and without doubt could not have been bettered anywhere. Amongst the award winners were American, Russian and South African performers.

At the conclusion of this wonderful experience we were escorted to the legendary Monte Carlo Casino where, for a few hours, we played the gaming tables. Some of our party spent rather more than they should have done, but I have always been cautious where games of chance are concerned, so my losses, fortunately, were modest. Not surprisingly, none of us broke the bank at Monte Carlo, as the famous song declared! We returned to our hotel in the early hours of the morning, and, a little merry from the fine food and wines we had enjoyed, retired for what remained of the night.

The following day was memorable in its own way, as we were taken to a number of remarkable places, but that night has never faded from my memory, even if I didn't meet the Grimaldi family personally. At the end of the trip we were each presented with an exclusive scarf memento which I still treasure and wear on special occasions in the company of friends.

Heather at Weston Park

The scene of Henkel's next surprise was rather closer to home, as Heather and other club members' wives were invited to join us for a weekend stay at Weston Park, the magnificent Shropshire home of the Earl of Bradford. The house is an architectural masterpiece set in spectacular grounds and has been in the Bradford family for generations. It was a favourite retreat of former British prime minister Benjamin Disraeli, who said of it: 'You will find Weston beautiful. I marvel whether I shall ever see the like of it again.'

During the weekend club members enjoyed lavish hospitality in most elegant surroundings and took part in a range of activities, including clay pigeon shooting. For weeks afterwards my right shoulder ached from the recoil of the gun, but the discomfort was insignificant when set against the pleasure of being in such a wonderful place.

Rob Jenkins, the general manager of Henkel, had overall responsibility for promoting and organising all the Henkel Executive Club events, and I have not yet mentioned the fine taste he had in food and wine. This ensured that the dining experiences on our special days were always extremely memorable.

Two in particular stand out in my mind, and were so exceptional that I find it almost impossible to offer an opinion on which was better. The first was a remarkable meal in Le Manoir aux Quat'Saisons, the restaurant of the renowned chef Raymond Blanc, set in the lovely countryside of Oxfordshire. The meal was almost beyond description, its delicate flavours and exquisite presentation causing me to think that if I never ate again, the food we had eaten that night would serve as my most treasured memory of a meal. Raymond was the perfect host as he walked around shaking hands with each of us individually at the end of the evening.

The second outstanding dining experience occurred when club members were taken to the London restaurant owned by the famous chef Anton Mosimann. There was an almost palpable atmosphere in the place, which I believed must have been created by the many famous celebrities, titled diners and others who had been overjoyed with what they had eaten, and had left their thoughtful appreciation behind before going home. However, I was soon to discover that there was another, surprisingly different component to this lovely atmosphere, of which I only became aware after I had met Anton and thanked him for an unforgettable experience.

Rob Jenkins approached my table and asked if I had enquired about the origins of the lovely building in which we were dining. I told him I hadn't, for in the mellow glow that followed such an outstanding meal, I had given little if any thought to the history of the premises.

'Well,' he said. 'I thought you might be interested to know that this place used to be a Spiritualist church.'

No surprise, then, that there was such a wonderful atmosphere present in the building!

* * * *

In 1989 Heather and I set off on a long-planned trip of our own. We were always eager to learn more of the cultures and customs of other nations, and had decided to travel to the Far East. We also had another very special reason for making the journey – my brother Bert, who had been killed on active service in 1946, was buried in the local cemetery, and I had wanted all my life to visit his grave.

We spent the first three days in Singapore, which proved delightful. The cleanliness and tidiness of the streets and leisure spots left us full of admiration for the way the local services operated. The friendliness of the people also made a great impression on us and added so much to our experience. Food was a particular pleasure for us, and we enjoyed some excellent meals, particularly in the city's Chinese quarter. We also took the opportunity to visit the home of the legendary Raffles, a society gentleman and accomplished jewel thief. His furniture and possessions were being sold off and we were curious to see what was there. That visit was to some extent a disappointment, since most of the good things had already been sold and the place was virtually empty.

Being anxious to visit the harbour where, in 1946, my brother Bert's Sunderland flying boat had crashed into the sea, I asked our taxi driver, the same one who had collected us from the airport a few days earlier, if he knew anything about the wartime events which had taken place there. He amazed us with what he knew about the crash, and offered to take us to the harbour the following day.

True to his word, he drew up outside our hotel first thing the next morning. We climbed into his car and set off on our journey. Though the harbour where Bert had died was our ultimate destination, the driver took us to various places of interest on the way. It was quickly evident that we were in a country of sharp contrasts, traditional Buddhist shrines juxtaposed against a commercial district which was becoming ever more prominent in the international money markets. Our driver also made a point of showing us a traditional Chinese funeral, in which we were able to become involved. It was a very moving experience, but also a happy one, since the bereaved family were simply content to wish their deceased loved one a joyful journey into her next life. Huge and elaborate floral displays were arranged around the open coffin, and we followed at the back of the procession for a short while, showing solidarity with the mourners.

Later, as we approached the precise spot in the harbour where Bert's plane crash had taken place, Heather and I grew quiet. It was forty-three years since he had passed on and I had always hoped that one day I would be in a position to visit the place where it had happened. Now, here we were.

The driver must have sensed our emotion, for he soon broke down in tears himself and cried for several minutes, something I found very touching. Heather and I got out of the car and stood on the harbour, looking out to sea. It was an extremely emotional moment for me, as I imagined the events that had taken place on that long ago day. If only the plane had taken off a little earlier, I thought to myself, or even just risen a little higher, Bert might still be here. We had been so close, and I regretted terribly that we had not been able to share life's experiences together.

It was hard to tear ourselves away from a place we had waited so long to visit, but at length we climbed back into the car and headed to the nearby cemetery where Bert's grave was located. In one of life's extraordinary synchronicities, the driver revealed that the grave next to Bert's was that of a soldier whose family lived just three miles from our home in Stourbridge, and whose aunt was one of our church members. On our return home, we lost no time in telling her what we had discovered. She was overjoyed to think that we had been able to pay our respects to her nephew.

A day or two later we flew to Bali in an old plane so rickety and shaky that it would have frightened the life out of a faint-hearted flyer. Arriving at our hotel, however, we found it to be almost the last word in luxury, and it was only on the third day that we ventured beyond its precincts. The outside world was in complete contrast to the Western-style comforts we had been enjoying – a contrast so marked that we never forgot it.

Setting off on foot, we walked along the dusty roads and were welcomed by family after family in a most sincere and friendly manner. Since it was approaching lunchtime, one family, whose father was a teacher and spoke English, bade us sit down and partake of their simple meal. Their generosity and kindness always remained with us, as did their custom of placing a small plateful of food in a specially designated area so that their spiritual guardian (God's messenger) would be symbolically involved in the joy of sharing food provided by the source of all life.

Many of our days in Bali were spent exploring the simple, humble culture of its people. In this respect we were very fortunate to make friends with a man who became our guide, and because of our interest in things other than the traditional holiday pursuits of lying in the sun or swimming, he took us into the interior of the island to locations most tourists never glimpsed.

We visited a number of shrines and temples, and were also taken up into the mountains to see a huge volcano at close quarters. Standing at its very edge, peering into the deep abyss, was to some extent frightening, but it was a unique experience, and one we would not have missed.

One the way back to our hotel that evening, we stopped at a place where a group of men were to walk on the traditional hot coals. I had seen this done once before at Stansted Hall, but it bore no comparison. At Stansted, the man who had done it had been on and off the coals in a flash. Here, we saw the bed of coals being carefully prepared, about five feet long and glowing red in the gathering dusk. Stepping onto them, the walker proceeded across at a sedate, dignified pace, with no rush at all. It seemed that for him it was not just about walking on the coals, it was almost an act of reverence and respect, as if paying obeisance to a deity.

We felt privileged to have experienced places and events which gave us such a unique insight into the traditional Balinese way of life. They left an indelible mark on our spiritual outlook.

* * * *

Returning home, the religious traditions of the Far East were still very much in my mind as I set about preparing for a rather unusual Divine Service at Stourbridge – unusual, because it would be broadcast nationwide.

I have already mentioned that on a number of occasions I had the opportunity to put the case for survival after death on both radio and television. Some of these programmes were challenging; others required considerable patience, and none more so than the live radio phone-ins in which I took part. Occasionally a caller would phone with very biased views and, when I tried to answer their point, would quote endlessly from this or that religious book. Almost without exception it was apparent that such people had never read the wealth of material contained in books by greatly respected writers on our subject. To such callers Spiritualism was a dirty word and no matter what reasoned argument was put forward, they were determined not to hear it.

One particularly extreme example of this occurred when, just minutes before the start of a radio broadcast from the

BBC's Pebble Mill studios in Birmingham, I was told that a Christian clergyman would oppose me on air. It was the first intimation I had been given of this gentleman's involvement. He was carrying a large Bible with lots of markers sticking out of the top, and seemed delighted when he saw that I was unprepared with a similarly marked volume to offer counter-quotes. He also stated that he planned to speak out most strongly about recent press attacks on the integrity of Gordon Higginson. These reports had been vicious and a cause of great distress among Spiritualists who knew Gordon to be one of our very finest mediums.

At this statement the blood rushed to my head and I told the reverend gentleman in no uncertain terms that if he went ahead with this lie, I myself would speak on the recent allegations concerning the shameful behaviour of some Christian clergymen in relation to young children. He immediately urged me not to do so, and the final outcome was that neither of us followed this adversarial course.

The programme shortly to be filmed at Stourbridge, however, was to prove a notable contrast to such prejudice. Entitled *Giving up the Ghost*, it was presented with relative honesty and fairness, and focused upon Gordon Higginson and myself.

The following extracts from a *Psychic News* report, which appeared a week after the broadcast, are indicative of reaction to the programme, which was presented by the respected anthropologist, Nigel Barley. Until I came across the article myself, I had not realised just how many people were reported to have seen the programme.

Nigel Barley

Millions of Britons saw Spiritualist minister Eric Hatton speak of his survival conviction on TV last week.

In TVS' 'Native Land' series Spiritualists' National Union president Gordon Higginson was also seen demonstrating clairvoyance at Stourbridge National Spiritualist Church in the West Midlands.

Anthropologist Nigel Barley – who assists Sir David Attenborough – attempted to 'discover the way the British deal with death.'

His programme, 'Giving up the Ghost', featured cremation, a team of crusading evangelists and 'practitioners of a rather curious cult. They concern themselves with violent death on an instrument of torture, childbirth outside wedlock and their principal ritual is a mass cannibal feast. They call themselves Christians.'

Mr Barley's first stop was at a Birmingham Church of England. 'To be Christians,' he told viewers, 'we have to believe in it, even if we don't know exactly what we are believing in.'

After talking with clergy, evangelists and undertakers, the anthropologist asked: 'What of the spirit? Some religions have very clear ideas, even a guarantee. Should you have doubts, they will give you a demonstration.'

Viewers then met Minister Eric Hatton, president of Stourbridge church and SNU vice-president.

The minister began: 'I have established to my own satisfaction that life after death is a fact, and that people, when they die, no matter what their belief may be – whether they have a faith of any order or not – scientifically they survive.' Snippets of Gordon's clairvoyant demonstration at the church were shown. The congregation's bright faces clearly indicated the accuracy of his mediumship, though TV viewers did not hear all the evidence.

Eric explained to viewers that the 'etheric body, which is invisible to our physical sight, operates on a vibratory level that only people who are gifted – who have what used to be termed second sight – are able to see. But that isn't a thing they can see all the time; that isn't something coming to them every moment of the day. It is only glimpses they have from time to time.'

One of Gordon's messages concerned a little girl who had grown up in the spirit world. The woman recipient, close to tears of joy, acknowledged this. Then Gordon spoke of communicators who 'saw you doing something with a tree today. You have been out in the garden.' This applied to her friend, sitting beside her, testified the woman.

Though viewers were left in the dark, the significance was explained to PN later.

'This was evidence!' said Eric. 'The woman had been planting a tree that day in memory of someone. The detail Gordon gave her was very good indeed.'

Next, Gordon told a woman of a male communicator who 'wanted to thank her for being patient with me for so long.' He was ill for some time before his passing, the medium added. The message was acknowledged.

Later, Eric told PN that he had known the communicator for some years and had conducted his funeral. He added: 'Gordon could not possibly have known the details of the manner of his passing, the suffering and treatment he had in hospital, and various personal details about him which were conveyed to his wife. She was very appreciative.'

Media critic Peter Rhodes reviewed the programme.

He wrote: 'By far the most impressive character in this essay was Eric Hatton, minister of the National Spiritualist Church in Stourbridge. He declared thoughtfully, quietly and quite frankly that the afterlife was a fact and that he would one day be reunited with his loved ones.'

PN asked Eric for his views on the programme. He explained that the TV crew had spent half an hour interviewing him at his home.

'They asked me quite a lot of questions,' he said, 'some of which were more pertinent than some of those presented. I just confirmed my absolute assurance that we meet again after we pass away.'

Asked if he felt Spiritualism's case was presented fairly, Eric replied: 'Yes. They weren't in any way critical. My only concern was that I regret that they didn't give it enough coverage, both in time and some of the startling evidence Gordon Higginson gave in the church.'

Nigel Barley later told Eric how impressed he was with the Stourbridge service.

Tim Rayner, who both produced and directed the TV programme, sent Eric a letter of thanks.

'Your courage in tackling difficult subjects head on,' he wrote, 'is what has given this series its sparkle and ultimately its wit.'

It was only in recent times that my attention was drawn once again to the programme *Giving up the Ghost*. The above report had slipped my memory and the praise it contained caused me some embarrassment.

However, I do realise the significance of the programme, in that it did not contain the bias which had been displayed in previous television programmes in general and by the BBC in particular. None of these broadcasters had been inclined to allow a balanced presentation of Spiritualism, less still to permit the broadcast of a Spiritualist service. This programme, therefore, was to some extent a breakthrough.

Chapter 11

The end of an era

A test of friendship ✦ *A sporting weekend* ✦ *The passing of Gordon Higginson* ✦ *Birth of the J.V. Trust*

My duties as vice-president of the SNU, and of course as a minister, continued to occupy much of my time. Unlike other religious organisations whose ministers are paid a stipend, those of the SNU carry out their work on a voluntary basis, at best being reimbursed for their expenses. The role of the president of the Union is no different, but the expectation of him or her travelling to venues, churches and special events can be very much more demanding, particularly if the person concerned has mediumistic talents. Such was the case with Gordon Higginson, whose mediumship was exceptional and therefore in constant demand.

I have often marvelled at how he managed to fulfil all these roles. He simply did not know how to say 'No' and would invariably acquiesce when he was prevailed upon to demonstrate his mediumship or carry out presidential duties around the country. The strain upon him must have been very considerable.

There were many times when, as his vice-president, I would have to stand in for Gordon in one capacity or another. I have never been able to establish for certain whether or not at times he arranged certain things to put me on my mettle and test my ability to take over from him at very short notice when, for instance, he found himself double-booked with commitments many miles apart. These included chairing National Executive Committee meetings, meetings of the council, and carrying out other functions, sometimes at the last minute.

One such occasion which really concerned me was when Gordon phoned at 9.30 one evening to ask if I would conduct a marriage service at 11.30 the following morning. A little flustered, I protested, 'But the bride and groom will need a rehearsal,' adding that they would be shocked to see me standing there, waiting to conduct their wedding, when they were expecting to see him.

'Oh, don't worry,' said Gordon matter-of-factly. 'I rehearsed them earlier this evening and they'll be quite happy when they see how well you conduct the service.'

What confidence he had in me! I, however, was uncertain I shared that confidence, and all the more so when I learned on arrival at Longton Church that Gordon had rehearsed the couple using the Greater World Service Book and I was about to conduct the service from my SNU Ministers' Handbook!

As things turned out, all went well and the couple were happy. Even so, a day or two later I confronted Gordon about the position he had placed me in. He was unabashed and said airily: 'Eric, I had every confidence that you would do it well. It's all good training for you.' What a test of our friendship!

On 28th April 1990 Gordon was contributing to a seminar at Torquay, in Devon, when, out of the blue, he suffered a minor stroke. He made light of it, and at the seminar's conclusion drove his car to Weymouth to play a principal role in another such event. Since he was engaged upon this task, I had in his absence been given the honour of re-dedicating Bournemouth Spiritualist Church. At the conclusion of the ceremony Heather and I drove to Weymouth to link up with the seminar and with Gordon.

On our arrival we found him in the process of delivering a talk to the assembled audience and were deeply shocked to see his condition. From previous experience in my own family I immediately recognised that Gordon had suffered another stroke. With the agreement of the seminar organiser, Mrs Sadler, I halted the talk immediately and led Gordon away to the chalet in which he was staying. We called a doctor who had no hesitation in diagnosing a stroke.

Over the next two days in that seaside chalet we nursed Gordon as best we could, and the doctor, who paid several visits, eventually agreed to allow him to travel in our car to Stourbridge where, in our home, he was nursed for two further weeks.

He had lost function in some areas of his body, but, for him, there had been a far greater loss: it seemed that his mediumistic gifts had deserted him. This caused him absolute despair and he feared that the loss would be permanent.

The days passed, and one morning I visited his room to deliver an early cup of tea. I was greeted by a highly emotional Gordon, who explained that my mother had appeared clearly to him and spoken words of encouragement. 'My gift is back!' he cried. Heather rushed to the room and we all three embraced with unmeasured joy.

Two weeks later he walked slowly to the car of his friend Paul Jacobs, who had come to collect him. Reaching out his hand to Heather and me, he said, 'Your love and nursing, together with the music you have played for me, have saved my life. I will never forget the healing you have both given to me day and night.' We were truly humbled by these words.

* * * *

Welcome relaxation came in the form of a weekend conference at Brocket Hall in Hertfordshire, one of England's finest stately homes. Along with a number of others, Heather and I were guests of the Bostic company – makers of Blu-Tack and other adhesive products.

Over three hundred years old, Brocket Hall has been the home of two British prime ministers, played host to King George IV, and witnessed the celebrated socialite Lady Caroline Lamb introducing the waltz to England in its spectacular gilded ballroom.

The house is situated in 543 acres of beautifully maintained parkland, boasting a huge lake, a magnificent Palladian bridge and a world-class golf course. Inside, it is filled with a breathtaking array of paintings and rare antiques, all displayed within some of the most beautiful rooms I have ever seen. From its spectacular grand staircase to its frescoed ceilings and wood panelling, it can only be described as a feast for the eyes.

Our conference was, among other things, intended as a team-building exercise and over the weekend I and my fellow guests took part in a variety of competitive events, including archery, land-buggy racing and clay pigeon shooting. This last I avoided like the plague, following the earlier shoulder injury.

Snooker was also on the menu, under the guidance of Jimmy White, who was then in his late teens and already a rising star in the sport. Although I had played a few games of snooker in the company of my brother Bert when we were teenagers, I never had a great deal of aptitude for it in the way that he did, and therefore took little interest in the game as it became increasingly popular during the 1980s and 90s. Because of this I knew almost nothing about Jimmy until I found myself part of the small competitive team at Brocket Hall. He was a shy lad, who I imagine must have felt a little ill at ease in the company of us, his older followers.

The sporting events done for the day, a traditional gala dinner was scheduled for the evening, but beforehand we had the opportunity to meet the house's owner, Lord Brocket, who took very considerable pride in showing us the specially designed building constructed to house his famous collection of Ferraris – twenty-four of them, all in gleaming red. Their value must have run into millions, but little did any of us suspect that his lordship would later use those cars as a means of raising funds to support his lavish lifestyle.

Some time later, I read in the papers that he had attempted to defraud the cars' insurers of spectacular sums of money. The police investigation was very high-profile and resulted in many of the cars being found at the bottom of the huge lake on his estate. Lord Brocket was sent for trial and was convicted of conspiracy to defraud his insurance company. He served a two-and-a-half year sentence in seven different prisons. Stylish and unconventional as ever, on completing his sentence he left prison amid a blaze of publicity, roaring away on a Harley Davidson motorbike!

Though he now lives a more conventional life as a London-based architect, Lord Brocket still owns Brocket Hall, which is now estimated to be worth about £42 million. It is currently leased to a German consortium.

* * * *

At a reconvened SNU conference in Manchester, in the summer of 1991, Gordon astounded everyone when at the evening public meeting he demonstrated his mediumship almost to his normal high standard.

In the eighteen months following the conference he kept faith with the many commitments already in his diary before travelling to serve Blackpool Spiritualist Church in January 1993. Concluding his duties there he made his way home to Longton to be greeted by his sister-in-law Elsie. 'Would you like a cup of tea?' she asked him. 'Yes, please,' he replied. She went into the kitchen to make the tea, and as she was doing so, heard a thud. Hurrying out to the corridor she found him on the floor. His earthly work had come to an end.

I was soon contacted with the news, which shocked me deeply, as also did the next statement: 'You are now our president.' Under the Union's rules it was accepted procedure that the vice-president would take over in the event of the incumbent president passing while in office. Thus I took on the presidency until the next SNU annual general meeting in July, at which an earlier postal election confirmed me as president for the next year.

Gordon's funeral service took place on 27th January 1993 and was an occasion at which great sadness was mixed in equal measure with a celebration of his remarkable life. It was

Gordon Higginson 1918-1993
President of the SNU 1970-1993

held in Longton Spiritualist Church where he had been president for several decades, and was attended by so many people that the church itself and the very large school room downstairs plus every conceivable room and space were packed to capacity. Many had to stand outside in the rain.

I was honoured and privileged to conduct the service, and in my tribute to his seventy-four years of life, twenty-two of which were spent as president of the SNU, no matter how much I tried I knew I could never pay sufficient compliment and tribute to him, nor indeed sum up the devoted service and mediumistic talents of such a great man. In trying to illustrate some of his exploits and achievements there were moments when I became emotional, but my determination not to let him down helped me to take a grip on myself, for I knew that he was present.

Afterwards, Heather and many others told me that my emotion had caused them to shed their own tears; nevertheless my duty was to carry all those present upon a journey of celebration for his life, his laughter, his complete devotion to the spirit world, his love of music and his determination to create happiness in the lives of others.

Many people had travelled long distances to be present at the service. Those representing other bodies and organisations mixed with the masses of folk who lined the streets outside as the cortège proceeded to the crematorium. No amount of rain could have prevented them from paying tribute, each in their own way, to a unique soul.

* * * *

From a personal point of view, I was acutely aware that it was now my duty to follow the exceptional Gordon Higginson as president of the SNU. My eight years of being his deputy had to some extent prepared me for this difficult task, but even so I felt inadequate, and though Gordon had once told me that I must be my own person, my awareness of my own shortcomings frequently caused me to have sleepless nights.

Just a few weeks before Gordon's death I had acceded to his request, and those of Roy and Christine Wandless, that I should become a trustee of the J.V. Trust which, at that time, was a modestly funded independent trust, established in memory of the couple's first two children, John and Valerie, who had passed from cystic fibrosis. Little did I or Hugh Davis, who had been appointed a trustee at the same time, realise that Gordon would pass so soon after we had signed the trust deed prepared by the Wandless's solicitor, Margaret Neville. Then, shock upon shock, just three months later Christine herself passed, followed a short time later by her husband Roy.

Miss Neville has remained a guiding light and wise advisor from that day to this. As the Wandless's solicitor it fell to her to unravel their complicated affairs. Little by little the situation became clearer, and to the great surprise of us all Miss Neville explained that by virtue of their legacy the trust would be in receipt of very considerable funds. I was

Roy and Christine Wandless

appointed chairman of the trust in 1993, and on Miss Neville's advice, Heather and Hugh's wife Margaret were also made trustees. When the need arose – which it certainly did – the four of us were able to assist the Arthur Findlay College in overcoming many problems. Prime among these was a health and safety closure order placed upon it in 1993, which would have shut the place down had it not been for the provision of money by the J.V. Trust.

Over subsequent years the trust has provided funds for a multitude of improvements, including new bedrooms in the old quarters of Stansted Hall; a newly created dining room and state-of-the-art kitchen; the dismantling of crumbling old chimneys and their subsequent reconstruction; the renewal of a roof which had become dangerous; the replacement of rotting window frames with new double-glazed oak substitutes; new windows and doors to the Sanctuary; replacement stone structures; partial re-leading of the Pioneer Centre roof; construction of an entirely new bar; staff toilets and shower room; a séance room in the basement of the building (now unused and abandoned); a loft conversion; provision of private reading rooms; and most recently, in 2009, £220,000 in part-purchase of land surrounding the college.

The trust has also made substantial contributions to the laying of a new access road to the Hall and also to the pathway from the Sanctuary area through the garden to the SNU headquarters, Redwoods. Redwoods has also benefited from re-roofing and other refurbishments and work has been undertaken to update the bedrooms in Clock Cottage – part of the original stable block belonging to the Hall. Funds have also been supplied for extensions to the Union's offices and its boardroom, along with contributions to re-establishing the historic market garden.

To enable the Hall to have a modern central heating system the J.V. Trust paid for a new gas main to be extended from the main road outside the estate. The formerly dreadful water supply system was abandoned and replaced with a safe, clean supply main which enabled us all to drink water without fear of illness, the old supply having necessitated our boiling water before we could drink it – a task which was to say the least unappealing when one needed a drink of water in the middle of the night.

Many other items provided by the trust have enhanced the charm and grace of Stansted Hall, not least of which were the contributions made to ensure that the Sanctuary was a most pleasant and peaceful place for visitors to enjoy. During the last sixteen years we have been able to provide life-saving funds for Stansted Hall, Stansted Estate, the SNU and a good number of churches. We have also made it possible for Spiritualists who could not otherwise afford to enjoy the experience of a holiday at Stansted Hall to do so cost-free during what has become known as J.V. Trust week.

In listing these things I have not done so boastfully, but rather to acquaint people with what has been accomplished through the foresight and generosity of Roy and Christine Wandless, which they and Gordon Higginson entrusted me and future trustees to carry out. Much of this work has been done with the co-operation of former SNU president Duncan Gascoyne, to whom I pay tribute. He has demonstrated considerable practical application in ensuring that necessary work has been undertaken, in addition to his major efforts to make the college financially viable.

In spite of these positive achievements by the trust, I, and to a lesser degree the other trustees, met with opposition and accusation at times. When we embarked upon the building of new bedrooms, the dining room, and the roof and chimney restoration, we engaged the building services of Barry Smith and his team, who each Monday would travel to Stansted from their base in Rowley Regis near Birmingham. They would stay for four nights each week in very basic caravan accommodation in the grounds of the Hall.

Barry had been engaged for his wide experience as a building overseer and his common-sense approach to all things pertaining to the building trade. Equally important was the fact that his charges were very considerably lower than those of more local firms which had tendered for the work. Nothing was too much trouble for Barry Smith's team and they were often called upon to carry out all kinds of remedial work that was not within their original remit.

While this work was going on, trouble was brewing behind the scenes. Those readers who know me may find it hard to believe, but a wholly unjust and insulting rumour was spread that I was benefiting financially in some way from the work which was being carried out. Barry Smith lived just a few miles from me in the Midlands and there was an implication that I might have received a 'backhander'. I still hold correspondence from the Union, collated by Margaret Neville, requesting that the J.V. Trust should no longer pay directly for the building work but should instead hand over the money, lock stock and barrel, to the college to disperse as they chose.

In answer to these accusations I state categorically that in all my years of involvement in the Spiritualist movement, and in this and many other ventures at Stansted Hall, I have never received one penny for anything I have done.

As trustees, we had envisaged further work being done at Stansted, for which the trust would pay, and with this in mind we had encouraged Barry Smith over the preceding months to expand his range of equipment, particularly scaffolding, so that he would not need to continue to hire such items from local companies at expensive rates.

At about this time, detailed plans were being drawn up by a local architect for an ambitious new project at Stansted – the building of a centre which would honour the pioneers of Spiritualism, to be known as The Pioneer Centre. It was to consist of one large room, a smaller healing treatment room, plus kitchen and cloakroom facilities. Mr Smith asked my opinion on whether or not he should tender for this job on the basis of the precise detail in the plans, since he felt that some of the work could be carried out in a slightly different way, without compromising on quality, yet increasing cost effectiveness.

I suggested to him that he should tender as specified but might also suggest to the vetting committee that there were a number of ways in which money could be saved on the project. However, as things turned out he was never given the opportunity to do so, since without further reference to him the contract was awarded to a building firm from Hertfordshire. Mr Smith was instructed forthwith to remove his caravan, which had been sited in the area where work on the new Pioneer Centre was to begin.

The passage of time revealed that the Hertfordshire firm was distinctly dubious; much of the work carried out was shoddy – a fact confirmed by another independent building company, Bob Black Ltd. Despite this, the firm failed ever to return to make good their shoddy workmanship, and shortly afterwards went into liquidation.

His services no longer required by his prospective employers, Barry Smith, his team and their equipment returned to Rowley Regis. It was only then that they discovered that their contacts in the Midlands area had all but dried up due to the extended period they had been employed at Stansted Hall. A short while later Barry had no alternative but to liquidate his company, Heimarc. To a large extent I have blamed myself for all that transpired at that time, and have found it hard to forget.

* * * *

During my three years of office there were many very difficult decisions to be made, some affecting churches in various parts of the country. Most serious among these decisions were the precarious financial positions of both the Union and Stansted Hall. There were also difficulties concerning Redwoods. Because of the Union's financial problems the London Headquarters Fund had advanced money against the building, and also against Clapham and Grantham churches. Certain members of the LHF were decidedly hostile to these arrangements and were pressing the Union for repayment.

During a NEC meeting this became a pressing issue and I asked if I might leave the room in order to consult with my fellow trustees of the J.V. Trust. When I returned I was able to announce that we would provide funds to release the Union from this stranglehold. A delighted NEC cheered this news, since a very worrying situation would now be swept away. Stansted Hall, which had been closed by the local health and safety office for falling short of compliance in a number of areas, was for a while a nightmare. The building of new bedrooms and other essential work was crying out for funds. The J.V. Trust was the saviour to all these problems and I will never be able to thank Roy, Christine and Gordon sufficiently for setting it up.

Another problem which gave me sleepless nights was that of the Guild of Spiritual Healers in our churches. For the previous few years a degree of conflict had existed between some church committees and the Guild. This was not necessarily the fault of the Guild as such, but rather of certain of its leaders and members. Since this volatile situation could not be allowed to continue, there being the danger of more serious problems within the Union, it was decided that the Guild should be disbanded so that healing in our churches would thenceforth be carried out under the auspices of the church committee under the overall guidance of a national committee. I was called many names for instigating this step but time has proved it to have been the right decision.

Problems beset the Union and my 1994 presidential address to the AGM at Southampton was challenging. It appeared in *Psychic News* under the headline 'President's astonishing address shocks AGM delegates'. The paper reported that I had been made aware of irrefutable spirit messages which warned of a conspiracy intent on tearing apart the SNU. More than 900 members were present as I explained that a few months earlier, within the space of just a few days, I had received separate pieces of an alarming jigsaw of communication through three different mediums. These indicated an orchestrated plan by outside bodies who were opposed to our truth and were determined to wreck our work. Worse, they pointed to a conspiracy involving some within our own movement. I added that, had these messages come from Gordon Higginson alone, I would perhaps have held reservations, but so many of our illustrious predecessors had added their voices to the communications that I had no alternative but to accept them as true. I also pledged to defend myself against accusations from those who said I was a 'dictator', and I challenged false statements which alleged that I and the NEC were indulging in witch-hunts and holding kangaroo courts. Times were tough and the stress was considerable. I was heartened, though, when Dorothy Hudson, who was chairing the AGM, announced to delegates that I had been voted in as president by what she described as 'an overwhelming 83 per cent'.

* * * *

By 1996 I had become more conscious than ever of the health problems which were causing me increasing pain and difficulty in walking, restricting my ability to sleep for more than a few hours at a time and affecting my general health and well-being. In addition to my SNU duties I was still heavily occupied as managing director of my own company and with my continuing chairmanship of Key Consortium. I was also immersed in various local and national charitable activities, one of them being the Council of Faiths. Another – Spiritualist Aid – raised money for many projects, including one to provide water supplies for 22,000 people (so Oxfam told me) in Rwanda.

I was also a trustee of the Sally Ferguson Trust. Sally had been a greatly respected and gifted medium, a very humble person. During her life she brought many people joy and assuaged their grief by the contacts she brought them from their loved ones in spirit life. On one notable occasion she demonstrated her mediumship during a large public meeting in Birmingham at which the famous physicist Sir Oliver Lodge was the speaker. On a personal note, Heather and I were privileged to sit in a development group with Sally – just the three of us – for ten years.

In earlier times Sally, Heather and I had carried out a number of spirit 'rescues'. On one particularly wet and windy night we arrived at Sally's and almost immediately she asked us if we would take her to a place near Cannock and Rugeley in Staffordshire, some twenty-two miles away. A young couple were experiencing strange phenomena in their home and had been prevailed upon by their parents to invite Sally to investigate in the hope that she could discover what was causing the problem.

We set off immediately. The driving conditions were not too good as the rain was coming down heavily. Arriving at the cottage we introduced ourselves to the young couple. No sooner had we crossed the threshold than we were all three instantly aware that the atmosphere inside the small house was not pleasant. Little by little we began to pick up on things that might be contributing to the situation, but then Sally said: 'Someone has been killed here. It was an old lady and she was murdered.'

Well, it transpired that the old lady's son had murdered her for the money which she had tucked away underneath her bed.

She had always refused to allow him to go into her bedroom, obviously feeling uneasy about his discovering the money. What a poor atmosphere there was in that house.

We later learned from the young couple that after our visit all unwanted activity had ceased. They were able to live happily in the house for another year before moving to live in Australia.

Before leaving, they gave us confirmation of something we had strongly suspected but had been unable to verify. 'You know you asked us about any nearby water?' they said. 'Well, we've found out that in fact there is a well only a few feet from the house. It was covered over, so we had no idea it was there.'

This came as no surprise. We had visited various places in which there were hauntings, poltergeist activity and so on, and had almost invariably found that there was some kind of water source nearby, whether a well pumping water into the house, a watercourse or a canal.

People have asked me why this should be so. The only theory which makes sense to me is that water is a very strong conductor of electricity, and since it creates energy, that may be the reason why those who wish to manifest often find it easier to do so where there is water.

I have sometimes noticed that our mediums drink quite a lot of water during a demonstration. Indeed, some of them cannot really go more than a minute or two without taking a sip. Whether it is this which helps to stimulate the nervous energy required for communication, I do not know.

On another occasion we were contacted by a lady named Eileen Lewis, who was a member of Stourbridge church at the time. She was a very competent singer – a contralto – and her husband was the chief architect of the Dudley Municipal Authority, a prominent businessman in the area.

Locally, in grounds they owned, there was a fair-sized modern house which was rented out to students from a nearby college. Eileen had been alerted to the fact that in the middle of the night sheets and blankets were being ripped off the students' beds, and all kinds of other unexplained events were going on. She asked if Heather, Sally and I would pay a visit, which we agreed to do.

Well, whatever we did, it helped them and they had a degree of peace while they continued to live in the house, but in response to our question about a nearby water source they replied that they had no knowledge of one. Certainly there was nothing visible, and the house was modern. Nonetheless, and to her credit, Eileen Lewis made enquiries and discovered that there had been an earlier house on the same site. It had been demolished, but a nearby canal worker had apparently dug himself a well in the garden and subsequently it had been covered up.

I must say that I shudder when I hear of relative novices who, having been Spiritualists for just a couple of years or so, want to undertake rescue work. I think it is appalling, and have more than once reprimanded people for it. They have no training for such specialist work, and that is potentially dangerous, not only to them, but to everyone else involved.

* * * *

As I have already written, Sally passed on 18th December 1978, having suffered serious injuries in a car accident as she was being driven home after conducting a service at Bloxwich on 5th December. She was eighty years old. As a mark of respect for such a lovely lady, and following many requests, the Sally Ferguson Trust was established on 8th February 1980, with Gordon Higginson, George Cooper, Cissie Shaw, solicitor and local coroner John Edwards and myself as trustees. George had been a friend of Sally for many years. He was an accomplished speaker with extensive knowledge of Spiritualism and had often shared a platform with her. The objects of the trust were the furtherance of the religious philosophy of Spiritualism, the relief of sickness through spiritual healing and the promotion of education in matters of Spiritualism. Sadly, John Edwards passed in 1988 while working in court, and Heather was appointed a trustee in his place.

Spirit of Youth was also one of my projects. As its name suggests, it had been envisaged as a vehicle for young people to meet together, exchange ideas and carry out research. We also hoped that it might breathe new life into some areas of the Spiritualist movement. Since it was composed of younger people, with many calls on their time, some eventually dropped away as they took up other interests or became disillusioned in some way. This left mainly older people to make the idea work, and, though they were young at heart, they were perhaps not ideally suited to carry the message of spirit with the verve and charisma of the young. There was also the need to keep the project financially viable. In 2009 that aspect became paramount, and it was decided with great reluctance that Spirit of Youth should be disbanded.

In addition to all the foregoing responsibilities I had also been appointed a trustee of the Spiritual Truth Foundation and, with hindsight, I realise that I had perhaps taken on rather too much.

One weekend in August I was about to chair a National Executive Committee meeting at Stansted and was suffering from intense pain in my spine and head. A member of the NEC, who was suitably qualified, gave me treatment in a side room, and although this briefly improved my condition, within a short while the pain had returned.

As the meeting got under way we were discussing various matters when disagreement reared its ugly head and developed into a furious verbal battle between two members of the NEC, Duncan Gascoyne and Judith Seaman.

Coupled with the severe pain I was experiencing, and with my ever-present tiredness, I found this all too much, and when the meeting concluded late at night, as was almost always the case, I returned to my room in Clock Cottage with a heavy heart. I felt sick that this angry conduct had occupied our time and energy when we should have been engaged in constructive work for Spiritualism. Though I was tired out, sleep eluded me and I was restless, mulling over the evening's events.

Just before dawn I wrote out my resignation from the office of president and addressed it to Charles Coulston, the Union's General Secretary, for at that time, in a state of pain and exhaustion, I could see no way in which I might be strong enough to handle matters and act as conciliator in such a vexed situation. I returned home to Stourbridge in the early hours of Sunday morning.

The next day I was telephoned by Charles Coulston on behalf of the NEC. He asked that I return to Stansted Hall to discuss the matter of my resignation. During our conversation I told him that I had reconsidered my hasty decision and was prepared to withdraw my resignation in the interests of the Union.

In his customarily polite and courteous way, Charles listened to what I had to say and assured me that he would convey my words to the NEC and to the vice-president, Judith Seaman, who was chairing the proceedings in my absence. I told him that I would return to Stansted as he had requested. Heather decided to accompany me.

On arrival I was called in to meet with the NEC and put my side of the story. Having done so, I was asked to leave the room while the committee members deliberated. I did this without protest – after all, these were my colleagues with whom I had worked closely.

After a while I was recalled into the room, where Judith Seaman informed me that the NEC had discussed the situation and were not prepared to reinstate me as president. I was shocked. My biggest 'crime' had been to make a hasty decision of which only the NEC, Heather and I were aware. In the few hours which had passed since my letter had been received, no harm had been done to the Union and there could have been no wider repercussions from reinstating me.

In recognition of my services to the Union over many years – including eight as vice-president and almost four as president – I was asked if I would agree to accept the title of Honorary President of the SNU, whatever that meant. Heather and I discussed the matter at length and in the end I agreed to accept the gesture. Though the title was and still is a great honour, I have often questioned what it actually means in practical terms, since there were no criteria laid down for the role. Over subsequent years I have been asked again and again what lay behind the NEC's reluctance to reinstate me to the presidency but have been unable to give a conclusive answer. However, I have gleaned from members of that particular NEC that one of their number was asked to read out the by-law relating to resignation. Apparently it was considered binding, and a paper vote was taken, resulting in my resignation standing. How cruel are such rigid by-laws and those who unquestioningly abide by them chapter and verse.

In the fourteen years since that decision was made, people have pleaded with me to tell my side of the story, but I have always maintained that there should not be two fools when there needs to be but one.

Chapter 12

I don't believe it!

What an excuse! ✦ *La vie Parisienne*

Throughout the whole of our married life Heather had an innate desire to make people happy. She would frequently say that laughter was the best medicine anyone could prescribe.

Most of us put on a 'mask' to hide our true feelings from time to time, but when things go wrong it is not always easy to put on a happy face. Heather, though, was accomplished at this art.

She was never happier than when our children were joined by their cousins and other playmates, or when we had a house full of our wider family at the special parties we held on Boxing Days. Catering for twenty or more and at the same time keeping the children entertained was a source of great pleasure for her.

Our children remember, as I do, how she would burst into fits of spontaneous giggles at the antics of young and old alike. Within seconds her laughter would become infectious and she would have us all convulsed.

As we got older and were more frequently on our own, she would often start laughing at something I had said or done, or a memory of some friend would set her off. It was not that she was disrespectful of them but, like us all, they had little mannerisms which she would mimic.

Some people say a prayer at the end of the day, and we did too, but as we climbed the stairs on the way to bed we would often be in fits of laughter which would continue as we got into bed. There were times when Heather's laughter would be at my own expense, but it was usually not long before I saw the funny side of it and joined in the joke.

Since we always had our bedroom window open in summer or winter, I dare say many of our neighbours might have put their own interpretation on the giggles that drifted out into the street – but they would have been wrong!

A Henkel Club day-trip to France in 1990 gave Heather an ideal opportunity to tease me unmercifully...

I have often wondered what the reactions of other club members' wives were when, like myself, each had to telephone home to say that the engines of the plane we had boarded to return to England would not start. The propeller engines, which had to be turned over by battery, flatly refused to oblige, and though they may have sounded decidedly implausible, our telephoned excuses were absolutely true!

Astonishingly, the small airport at L'Ortolan had no other high-powered battery, and after ninety minutes of strenuous effort the French engineer concluded that nothing could be done. This meant we were effectively stranded, with no other plane available until the next day. None of us had expected to be in this situation and so had brought no pyjamas, toiletries, change of clothing, or even a toothbrush.

Some of the party were very anxious because they had important commitments the next day, but there was no alternative other than to accept the situation and make the best of it. The trip organiser Rob Jenkins and his team quickly arranged accommodation at nearby hotels and by some means or other managed to provide each of us with a toothbrush, toothpaste and shaving materials, for which we were most grateful.

The following morning, a replacement plane was flown out from England, enabling us to reach our homes some twenty-four hours later than planned. I imagine we all had some explaining to do to our partners. Heather questioned me in jest and on many occasions enjoyed telling our friends the story. 'A modern plane wouldn't start?' she would say incredulously. 'What kind of an excuse is that? What a story!'

In December 1996 Heather and I celebrated our fortieth wedding anniversary, and were delighted when, in spring the following year, Lisa and Jonathan surprised us with the news that they had booked us a trip to Paris.

With great excitement we flew off on the appointed day, landed safely at Charles de Gaulle airport and installed ourselves in a nice, central hotel close to the Arc de Triomphe.

On the Saturday evening of our stay, Heather mentioned that she would love to visit the Paris Opera, a spectacular and very famous building. I said that it would probably be closed on a Sunday, but she was still keen to go because she had seen photographs of its magnificent staircase and was eager to see the real thing for herself. So the next morning we decided to set off in search of it.

It was a Sunday, and although the Metro was running, the shops were shut and the streets virtually deserted. We thought we were heading in the right direction, but as we walked on and on for what seemed like ages, there was not a sign of the opera house. After a while we stopped and asked for directions, but most people couldn't understand us, since my French was not up to much and neither was Heather's.

Eventually we came across a fellow who spoke reasonable English and, no doubt with the best of intentions, he directed us along a particular route. Eventually we arrived at a large building, believing it to be the opera house, but it turned out to be the Opera Comique instead. It was completely closed up, so we approached a passer-by and enquired again about the way to the opera house.

Directions received, we set off once more, going quite some distance, until at last we were met with the long-awaited sight of the Paris Opera House. The outer doors were unlocked and we were able to get inside, catching a glimpse of the magnificent staircase Heather had so much wanted to see. It was spectacular – a sight never to be forgotten.

A lady was seated behind a desk in the foyer, and we approached her to ask if it would be possible for us to take a look inside the main auditorium where the operas were performed. She spoke quite good English and told us that unfortunately it was closed.

I explained that we had come all the way from Birmingham, in England, and had also walked a long distance that morning to get to the opera house. Hearing this, she relented a little and said that it might be possible for us to look around inside and at the top of the staircase.

All the doors to the auditorium were closed and there was no way we could get inside. I spotted a lady and asked her if it might be possible for us just to peep through one of the doors and have a quick look. Well, there was no one else about, so she kindly opened a door and we slipped inside, a little afraid that someone might reprimand us, or that the lady herself might be in trouble for allowing us to go in. Heather was absolutely thrilled, although we felt that seeing the place empty was not quite the same as seeing it packed with an audience.

Our mission accomplished, the lady locked the door again and we came happily down the stairs, holding each other's hand like silly young kids.

The grand staircase at the Paris Opera House

We went back to the desk to ask if there was a performance taking place that evening. The receptionist told us that there was, but all the tickets had been sold. She explained that the performance was to be given by a British group and was a combination of acting and opera. They would be singing in English, she said. At this, I asked her if she could possibly find us two seats somewhere or other – we did not mind where.

She thought for a moment and, making up her mind, said, 'We don't normally let out this box, but since you've asked and you've travelled so far, we'll let you have it this evening.' Needless to say, we were delighted, and so I duly paid for the tickets and we set off back to our hotel.

In the evening we arrived in good time and were shown into a box which fronted directly onto the side of the stage. We hadn't been seated very long when some of the cast started to come into the wings, and behind the curtain we could see along the passageway leading to the stage.

The performance was magnificent and the opera house packed; it was a most enjoyable and memorable experience. The whole event was such a special occasion for Heather that we decided to celebrate afterwards by going to a particularly nice restaurant. In true French style we took our time enjoying an excellent Sunday evening meal.

As we left the restaurant we enquired if there was a Metro train which would take us back to the Arc de Triomphe and were recommended to travel on the lower, deeper level of the Metro. Apparently, our station was only two stops away and the journey would be quick and easy. Little did we know!

Down we went to the lower level of the Metro and were on the platform for only a few moments before the train came along. After two stops we arrived at the Arc de Triomphe and proceeded to follow the crowd out, only to find to our absolute astonishment that all the barriers were closed. There were no staff in evidence and, much more worrying, there was absolutely no way we could get out of the station.

We were very anxious, having uneasy visions of being stuck there all night, but an English-speaking chap told us that if we wanted to get out we would simply have to climb over the barriers, which many people were already doing. Although I was seventy years old, I didn't mind doing this, but I wasn't sure that Heather was keen on the idea. Still, we had no alternative, so with the help of this chap I lifted Heather right over the top of the barrier. Fortunately, she landed safely on the other side and I followed.

By the time we arrived back at our hotel it was early morning. We had been quite worried, to say the least, at the thought of spending the night in the station, and Heather had been none too thrilled about our rather unconventional exit over the barrier. What an experience!

Later that morning we were having breakfast in the hotel dining room when a couple of uniformed gendarmes came in. 'Oh God,' we thought, 'we've had it now. We'll be arrested and taken off to prison!' The two policemen made straight for the head waiter, but to our great relief it transpired that they were talking about someone who had caused a disturbance in the hotel the previous night, and we were not about to be arrested. We were very glad indeed to have the incident behind us.

Heather still maintained that we should never have climbed over the barrier, but I pointed out that if we hadn't done so we would have been there all night. 'You do get me into some situations!' she said, adding that we should find some quiet, ordinary place to go to that night. I had other plans, however, and she relented when I told her that I had already made arrangements for us to take a boat trip for dinner on the River Seine. Both boat and river were beautifully illuminated and we had a most wonderful evening. Heather forgave me after that!

So that was our experience of Paris, on our ruby wedding anniversary when we were both seventy years old. Who would have thought that the Honorary President of the Spiritualists' National Union would be getting up to antics like that?

Chapter 13

Hard times

Trouble strikes ✦ *A glimpse of the next world* ✦ *A wonderful invitation*

With the dawn of the new millennium our business, which had thrived for so many decades, began to run into difficulties.

Macell, a company which was not a member of Key Consortium, had many wholesale warehouses around the country, and was selling greeting cards on a huge scale. Questions were raised as to how they would manage to finance this, because they had so many outlets. Eventually their indebtedness caught up with them and they owed several million.

There were two firms in particular, one named Simon Elvin, the other Fine Art, from whom we purchased greeting cards. Macell owed millions to Fine Art, and because of those debts, Fine Art agreed to act as principal in trying to solve the problem. They offered various warehouses to people like ourselves, but I was reluctant to go forward with the idea, although Jonathan and Lisa were favourably inclined towards it.

Frank Kerry, the founder of Fine Art, had been a good and trusted friend for many years. He was a respected businessman, well enough known that he had been the subject of TV's popular *This is your life* programme, an event in which I played a part.

* * * *

Back in the 1980s I had received a telephone call from a gentleman who asked if he could come to see me. He assured me his request was genuine and, though I was a little mystified, I agreed to it. The following day he came to my office, introduced himself and went on to tell me the purpose of his visit.

He was a producer of programmes for both BBC and ITV and had been engaged to produce a tribute to Frank Kerry. Since Frank and I had a business association going back to 1950, my visitor wanted to quiz me about him.

We talked for the better part of an hour, after which he told me how grateful he was. He then revealed that the programme he would be producing was *This is your Life, Frank Kerry*, and asked if I would be willing to take part in it. I agreed immediately.

A few days later he returned to confirm that the programme would be broadcast from the Grosvenor House Hotel in London's Park Lane. Heather was invited to accompany me. I learned that I was to be the first contributor on the programme, and for fifty minutes or so the gentleman rehearsed me on what he wished me to do and how he wanted me to do it, since I would be setting the scene for others to follow.

On the appointed day Heather and I travelled to London and were accommodated in a lovely room in the Grosvenor, with firm instructions not to venture anywhere near Mr Kerry's suite since the whole thing was a big surprise and therefore very hush-hush.

In the evening we were shepherded into the hotel's large and elegant ballroom and led to our table. We were asked to converse in hushed tones until Frank and his family arrived, then at a given signal the 100-strong crowd of guests would stand and applaud. The look of amazement on Frank's face as the applause erupted around him was a sight I shall never forget. I fancy that I saw tears in his eyes as he took it all in.

This is Your Life, Frank Kerry began with an outline of his journey from humble beginnings to his early success in business, after which I had to come out from behind a screened-off area. He was very surprised to see me and said so. I then spoke of our early association and of the help he had given me in setting up my own business. I was followed by a string of people, each of whom made their individual contribution. What a tribute it was to this man who had been behind so many philanthropic causes and helped such a variety of people in so many different ways.

After the show we enjoyed an excellent meal with a generous amount of wine. The producer went to Frank's table and offered thanks to his family for keeping the secret of the programme so well, which had led to such a splendid evening. He then produced a small tape player, saying to Frank that as a further tribute he would be playing a recording of the businessman's favourite type of music - 'Hooked on Classics'.

'I'll just push the play button, Mr Kerry, and away we go,' he said. With that the ballroom was filled with a wash of sound as the ten-feet-high silver curtains opened to reveal none other than the full 'Hooked on Classics' orchestra, complete with their conductor, Louis Clarke.

The atmosphere was electric, and became even more so when the orchestra went on to play Elgar's rousing Land of Hope and Glory. The whole place was awash with merriment, with some guests so enthusiastic that they climbed on to table tops to wave the flags which had suddenly been provided.

It was a night to remember, and in the years that followed Heather often spoke about it to our family and friends as being one of our finest and most enjoyable experiences.

* * * *

However, by the time Fine Art stepped in to address the problems affecting the Consortium, Frank Kerry had passed on, and a new leadership was in place. There was no longer the personal connection and friendship that had existed in former times.

Initially, Fine Art wanted us to take on a warehouse in Wolverhampton but we were reluctant to do so because, for various reasons, we didn't think it was quite the ticket. The other possibility was in Coventry, and was certainly the better of the two they had offered us. We wanted to take on Coventry, but it eventually boiled down to the fact that if we took one we would have to take the other, so we had no alternative but to take Wolverhampton as well. Of course the two warehouses had to be managed as satellites, and with hindsight I think that was a failing – we weren't tight enough on control.

Nevertheless, we decided to go ahead with the purchase of the warehouses, and Fine Art told us they would do the stocktaking for us in order to save us money. I thought that sounded good, and had no reason to doubt them. We fixed a price for the stocktaking and also signed up to an agreement whereby we would purchase many thousands of pounds' worth of goods from them each month. If we reneged, or fell short over a twelve-month period, we had to make up the quota. We also had to pay them rental for the leases on the premises.

After a while we realised not only that we had over-stocked the warehouses, but that a lot of the stock consisted of new designs we had not seen before. When Fine Art had tried out these designs on a pilot basis they had not been successful, yet they had put masses of them in both the Wolverhampton and Coventry warehouses, and probably in other places too. This left us in a difficult position; we had paid Fine Art £400,000 and had to try to negotiate a reduction on the amount of goods we were obliged to purchase, and on various other costs that were levied against us. Eventually we agreed on the sum of £300,000.

The matter of turnover also became an issue, though the facts were far from easy to establish. We discovered that, at the Wolverhampton warehouse in particular, goods had been moved in through one door, recorded as having been received, then sent out through another door and recorded as sales.

Unfortunately they had not been sold at all and had simply been moved to another warehouse. This, of course, gave a false impression of the figures, and in consequence the true turnover was nowhere near what had been claimed. Because we had such a massive amount of stock, and found that things were not moving as fast as we had expected, we began to develop a cash flow problem, given that we had to finance the constant monthly purchasing required by our agreement.

Heather and I put in a lot of our own money and I sold some shares and insurances and so on. What with these business problems, my chairmanship of the Consortium, and my many responsibilities in Spiritualism, the pressure on me was considerable and inevitably began to take a toll on my health. It was not long before those effects became all too apparent.

In 2001, as was their normal practice, Lisa and Jonathan travelled to Yorkshire for the Harrogate Toy Fair, an annual event at which toys and stationery were showcased.

During their absence I was in the office at Cradley Heath because Elaine, who had succeeded Cissie Shaw as secretary, was off sick. Feeling suddenly unwell, I collapsed beside her desk. Jennifer, who was working in the outer office, must have heard me fall, because she hurried over and said with concern, 'Are you all right, Mr Hatton?' I told her I would be fine, but she nevertheless went off and returned with a glass of water. She had also summoned Roger, the warehouse manager, so I suppose I must have looked ill. I certainly felt it.

I sat quietly on Elaine's chair for about three-quarters of an hour, trying to recover. Jennifer and Roger were keen to send for a doctor and an ambulance, but I wouldn't hear of it and eventually drove home. How I did so, I shall never know. I clearly remember that when I arrived home I sat down in an armchair with a hot water bottle laid on my chest; the pain was intense but the warmth was soothing. At that stage I did not know the cause of the trouble. I had been diagnosed with angina some years earlier, but wondered if perhaps this latest problem might signal something more serious.

Those events took place on a Monday, and by the following Thursday I was feeling very ill indeed. Later that day I suffered a heart attack and was rushed into Russells Hall Hospital in nearby Dudley. Dr Barr, the consultant, gave me a great deal of attention and eventually informed me that he had decided to transfer me to the Queen Elizabeth Hospital in Birmingham, a very large facility.

He had spoken by telephone with their senior cardiologist and surgeon, Mr Keogh, and now told me that although my case was urgent and they were very concerned about me, Mr Keogh did not know if he would be able to operate because he was due to fly to America the next morning in order to attend a conference.

Whatever the case, they shipped me off in an ambulance, accompanied by Heather and a doctor. Blue lights flashed as we sped through one set of red traffic lights after another, and when I reached the hospital I was admitted to a ward, following which an army of medical personnel descended upon me and began inserting tubes and carrying out other procedures with a view to an imminent operation. In the midst of all that frenetic activity, it seems that I must have died.

I later learned that the doctors had not taken any emergency action to resuscitate me, apparently believing it was all over. Well, to their amazement, I came out of it, but not before I had had a brief but extraordinary experience which I remember vividly to this day.

As clearly as if they had been physically present in front of me, I saw four people whom I knew very well: Harold Vigurs, Harry Edwards and Gordon Higginson, followed shortly afterwards by my father. They weren't dressed in white robes or anything unusual; they were just as I had known them. Of course Gordon had passed away a few years previously and I had first known Harry Edwards as a younger man, but my principal memories of him were as a man of about 70, and Harold Vigurs the same. My father had passed away at the age of 71. So all four men had presented themselves at approximately those ages for recognition purposes.

The whole scene was illuminated by brilliant colours, the like of which I would never have thought to see. The greens were so extraordinarily beautiful, indeed the whole spectrum of colours was overwhelming, impossible to put into words. Then finally my father put up his hands and said, 'Not yet. Not yet.' I could almost feel that he was sorry, that he would have liked me to join him, but he knew it was not my time.

I didn't experience the tunnel which so many people have described in near-death situations, but immediately after my father's words I came back to my body. The staff were amazed. To this day I can remember my element of regret that I couldn't stay in that place of such extraordinary beauty. In those seconds or minutes – I am unsure how long the experience lasted – I was so deeply impressed and affected by what I had seen that whenever I have subsequently spoken of it in Stansted Hall and other places I have become very emotional.

Following this dramatic sequence of events, I remained in the same ward, in a bed next to the nurses' station, and the care I received was wonderful.

At about six o'clock the next morning a man appeared at the foot of my bed. Seeing that I was awake, he greeted me and asked how I was feeling.

'I'm getting on all right,' I replied. 'I'll be OK now.'

At that, he said, 'You're very interesting to me.'

I still had no idea who he was, so I asked him. He answered that he was Mr Keogh, the surgeon. I had met him the day before of course, but had no recollection of it.

I was puzzled by his presence in my room, and said, 'But Dr Barr told me you were flying off to America.'

'I am,' he replied. 'I'm going straight from here to the airport, but you're such an interesting case that I've come to see you first.'

About an hour after that another man appeared by my bed and introduced himself as Mr Bonsor, also a consultant. He had brought one of his assistants with him, and explained that from what little he knew of my case he found it intriguing and had decided to come and see me even though, technically, I was not his patient.

As the day progressed, my cubicle took on the appearance of a busy thoroughfare as no less than seventeen doctors, anaesthetists and other medical personnel trooped in to see me, making a tally of twenty for the day. I was clearly something of a curiosity! One Chinese doctor visited me no less than three times that day and showed great interest in the experience I had had. He was frankly amazed that I had pulled through.

Throughout the time I was in hospital Heather struggled to visit me every day. It was many miles from our home and parking was difficult to say the least. Often Lisa or Jonathan would bring her, though she sometimes drove herself.

After eight days I was transferred back to Russells Hall Hospital, much nearer home, which made things a lot easier for my family. During almost ten days' recuperation there, I took the opportunity to respond to a rather strong letter I had received from Simon Elvin's financial director. I wrote that I did not think his attitude was justified considering all the business we had done with his company, and the fact that we had always paid them promptly. Simon, whom I knew quite well, replied personally to me, but there was nothing to be done.

I continued to build myself up and to try and regain some strength, and while still in Russells Hall, celebrated my 75th birthday. The next day, I was told that I was to be transferred back to Birmingham for triple bypass surgery.

Following the operation, which for medical reasons turned out to be a double bypass instead, I had to stay in hospital longer than expected because I developed an infection in my leg.

The surgeons had taken veins from the leg while performing the bypass, and although most of the staff were very particular about wearing gloves when dressing the wound, one young nurse used no gloves at all. The ward sister noticed this and gave her hell for it, but it was too late. The damage was done and the leg turned septic.

Eventually I was able to walk around a bit and was making my way slowly up a corridor near to the ward, when who should I see coming towards me but one of the sisters who, on that Thursday night when I had briefly died, had been on duty. She had gone on leave immediately afterwards and therefore had no idea of the events which had followed.

'Eric!' she called. 'How wonderful to see you!' She made a great fuss of me and explained that she had never expected to see me again.

'Why do you say that?' I asked her.

'Well, you were dead,' she said, not beating about the bush. 'We just gave up because there was nothing more we could do. I have to say it really upset me.'

Eventually, I left hospital and, with much relief, returned home. Lisa and Jon did not at first share with me their growing concerns about the business, bearing in mind that I had been in hospital for nearly three months and was still in the process of recovering from the ordeal.

Gradually, it became clear that the business was in a dire condition.

Apart from what had happened with the company which had sold us the goodwill, we also supplied a lot of people with Christmas goods on a large scale – specially printed cards, Christmas decorations and all manner of other items.

There was one particular firm with whom Jonathan and I had negotiated deals. They were called Autobar, and supplied hospitals, schools and other places with throwaway utensils and many other things. They had a huge distribution centre just outside Rugby in Leicestershire. We did good business with them and occasionally they would phone us and ask if they could have an item quickly. Sometimes it would be just one or two things and we would get them to them promptly.

One day, their buyer rang me up and said that he needed various items immediately. I pointed out that he had ordered those items the previous day and they were already on the van for delivery that day.

'I've already had them,' he told me.

'Well,' I said, 'it's only about 10.30am and they were ordered yesterday.'

He persisted, and said, 'This is a new order and I want it today.'

I explained that there was no way I could get the van back, as it was already on the road. But he was insistent, saying, 'Eric, I'm telling you, I want them today.'

The pressure was mounting and things were not looking good for us. Reluctant to disappoint him, I loaded up my car with what must have been a couple of thousand pounds' worth of goods and motored over to Rugby to deliver them. Because I knew the customers so well, I left the merchandise with them without signing their paperwork. Later, they would dispute that they had ever received the goods and never paid us a penny for them, although I had left them an invoice. Nor did they ever pay for a considerable amount of other goods which had been invoiced.

There were also some valued customers to whom I'd always given three or four months' credit – six months in some cases. Then I'd go along to them and point out that they'd had credit for some time and they would offer me a cheque immediately. It was a personal contact, which counted for a lot, and usually produced payment.

But although Jonathan and Lisa tried their utmost to persuade several other customers to pay us what they owed, they were not successful, and eventually liquidators were brought in. They, in turn, engaged a firm of London solicitors, which, on reflection, may have proved fatal.

Instead of the solicitors allowing us to make a direct personal approach to non-paying customers, they wrote a formal letter to each and every one. In some cases these letters were sent to customers who had always been loyal and paid us promptly – often within a week or so.

It was a matter of great regret to us that these people were dealt with in the same harsh way as those who had deliberately and consistently avoided paying, and some of them reflected back to Lisa and Jonathan that they had felt under considerable pressure. Lisa in particular gave a great deal of help to the solicitors, and one might have thought they would have allowed us to handle these particular customers personally, but they didn't, and so we went into liquidation.

When I think about it now, the amount of goods that were brought back to Cradley Heath from the other two warehouses was colossal, and the person who eventually bought them did so at an extremely low figure.

There was one other situation to resolve. We had a reciprocal agreement with the suppliers and two other members of the Consortium that we would sometimes have goods from them and they would have goods from us to balance things out. One was in Bristol and the other in the Midlands. We owed them money and owed them the goods. Heather and I paid several of them back out of our own money so they weren't left with a debt. I believe they always appreciated that.

At the end of it all we had contributed another £130,000, in addition to the considerable amount we had previously put in. And so it was that our business folded up after fifty years of trading.

* * * *

One evening in 2001, as I'd lain in hospital recovering from my heart problems, Heather arrived to visit me, as she did every night. On this occasion Jonathan had driven her and they brought with them a rather official-looking envelope which they thought might have come from some government official or other.

Opening it with a degree of curiosity, I discovered that it was an invitation to one of the Queen's garden parties at Buckingham Palace. Heather and I were overjoyed. I responded to it promptly, explaining that I was in hospital, but if my health permitted we would be delighted to accept the invitation.

Eventually, the day came for us to travel down to London for our long-anticipated visit to the palace. It had rained cats and dogs during the previous twenty-four hours but, to add to the pleasure of the day, the sun was shining brightly.

We drove south as far as Reading, where we stopped off at the home of my long-time friend and musical colleague Norman Morris and his wife Rosie. There, we changed into appropriate attire. Heather always had a very good dress sense, but on this occasion she excelled herself, wearing a most beautiful summer dress in a delicate shade somewhere between peach and magnolia, together with a most becoming hat. She looked a picture, and I was so proud of her. For my own part, I wore a traditional morning suit.

Dressed for the Queen

Decked in our finery we set off on the last lap of our journey to London. We parked the car in The Mall, not far from the palace gates. We then walked across to them, though they were locked because entry for Garden Party guests was via an entrance on the left-hand side of the palace. We quickly discovered that a dozen or so people had arrived before us.

By this time the day had become very hot,

and I was particularly conscious of the temperature since I was still regaining my strength after such a long period of ill-health. Nevertheless, having arrived so early, we had to stand in the sun for some time, as did the other people who were waiting with us. Amongst these were two fellows who let it slip that they were involved in the Northern Ireland legislature; this of course was at a time when things were not too good in Northern Ireland. They only painted a very general picture of the situation, but nonetheless it was a gesture of friendliness we appreciated.

Also standing with us were some Japanese people, complete with cameras. An official information letter had indicated to us that the use of cameras would not be permitted, so we had duly obeyed and not brought ours with us, but the Japanese visitors were snapping away like nobody's business!

Eventually, the gates were opened and we were ushered into the palace gardens, which are huge. Having already stood for such a long time in the sun, I realised that to sit out in the heat would be a very big test for me, so when Heather and I noticed a marquee we made a beeline for it. Luckily for us it was situated not far from one of the refreshment tents, so we sat down at a table and were soon approached by a couple who asked if they could join us. We readily agreed, and shared an interesting conversation while waiting for the refreshments to arrive. These consisted of sandwiches, laid out on silver trays, and filled with cucumber, cheese and a most tasty paste. A variety of cakes and other delicacies were also offered.

After we had eaten, Heather and the lady who had joined us remarked that they were keen to go and see the Queen in the Royal Park. Traditionally, guests are lined up there so that the Queen can stop from time to time to chat to somebody or shake their hand. So off they went, and I remained behind talking to the gentleman of the couple.

After we had chatted for what seemed like a long time, there was no sign of our wives, and I began to feel concerned, particularly since I wasn't sure Heather's geography was all that good. Fearing they might have got lost, I suggested to my companion that I should go off in search of them. Well, there were many hundreds of people there and I looked around and about and walked across the area from where the Queen was coming, but, try as I might, I could see no sign of them.

By this time, the Queen had passed through and I was walking backwards towards the palace when suddenly somebody jabbed an umbrella or stick in my back and said rather heatedly, 'Excuse me sir – you nearly bumped into the Duke of Edinburgh and knocked him over!' I think he may have sworn at me but I wasn't sure. Sure enough, I saw that I was indeed within a foot or so of the Duke. He didn't say anything to me.

Eventually I found Heather, although it's fair to say that I didn't actually find her. She had gone over to the other side of the gardens, about 150 yards away, where the Queen had entered a refreshment marquee after walking about and meeting a lot of people. Heather told me that Her Majesty had sat down in a chair and, no doubt relieved to be off her feet at last, had promptly kicked off her shoes. Heather was delighted with this occurrence and made great play of it!

I never knew quite why I was invited – it was said that the invitation was in recognition of 'services' but I did not know whether it was because of my involvement as a Spiritualist and as president of the SNU or for charitable services of some kind. Whatever the reason, it was a most enjoyable and unforgettable day.

Chapter 14

New horizons

*A unique opportunity for Spiritualism • A Methodist's sacrifice
for Spiritualists • The passing of Doris Collins • Quieter times*

It was in February 2001 that I had a telephone call from a
long-standing friend named Clive Lloyd, a Spiritualist and
minister of the SNU.

Clive was a local councillor in Cheltenham and had rung
to tell me that in all probability he would be elected mayor the
following May. He went on to make a most unexpected
request, asking if I would consider becoming mayoral
chaplain for his year of office.

I had resolved to take things a little more gently after such
a long period of illness and a number of thoughts went
through my mind, not least the distances I would have to
travel to fulfil the role. I also wondered how the council
would look upon the appointment of a Spiritualist as chaplain
when they were undoubtedly accustomed to having a
clergyman from one or other of the orthodox religions. I
voiced these concerns to Clive, but he was persistent, and at
length I agreed provisionally to undertake the duty, still not
knowing exactly what it would involve. Clive was pleased,
and we arranged to talk more about it nearer the time.

At the end of March he telephoned again and asked if I
was still willing to be his chaplain. I told him I was, and we
got straight down to the nuts and bolts of what it would
actually entail. He explained that I would first have to go to
Cheltenham to be sworn in as chaplain and thereafter would
have to go once a month to open the council meetings with a

prayer and a few observations. There were other functions during the course of the year, he told me, and I would be the principal representative at some of them. It was a nice prospect, I thought, and though I was not egotistical about it I felt it would be an interesting new experience.

When the time came for Clive's inauguration as mayor, Heather and I drove down to Cheltenham Town Hall to witness the traditional ceremony at which the previous mayor stood down and the new mayor – in this case Clive – took his place. It was quite an occasion, attended by mayors and mayoresses from neighbouring boroughs, along with other dignitaries and representatives of royalty.

A week or so later we set off for Cheltenham again, this time for the first council meeting and the start of my official duties. Arriving at the council offices, I was unsure about where I should leave the car, so headed to a car park at the back of the building. A gentleman was getting out of his own car as I pulled in, and he strode over to me with an air of authority and said firmly, 'You're not supposed to park here.'

I explained that I wasn't sure where I should park, but that I was the mayor's chaplain. At this he looked me up and down, and asked 'Are you sure?' I was dressed in a suit and wore no badge or anything else that might have identified me as a minister, so perhaps he thought I was an imposter! I suppose it was a slightly inauspicious beginning to my chaplaincy, but the gentleman soon backed down and invited us to follow him.

He led us through one of the rear doors, at which a commissionaire was stationed so that people could not wander in and out willy-nilly. I made myself known at the reception desk and was issued with an identification badge, after which we were shown through to the inner part of the building.

Heather went straight to the public gallery and I was taken to join Clive, his deputy mayor and the town clerk. Together, we went over the procedures for opening the meeting and shortly afterwards walked through the small doorway which led to the council chamber with its impressive mayoral 'throne'. I had been told that I should offer a welcome and a prayer, which I duly did.

Clive had already explained that I didn't need to stay any longer once I had done my part, but I felt that my short contribution didn't really amount to much for a mayor's chaplain, so I decided to stay on until break time, when council members stopped for a cup of tea and biscuits. Clive came over to chat with me and asked if I was going to stay for the second half of the meeting. 'It could go on for quite a long time,' he warned. I told him I would stay a little longer and then slip away.

Attending a council meeting, with its various opposing political factions, had been a new experience for me, and I thought it had been reasonably cordial. But at subsequent meetings it became more and more evident that fiery exchanges could develop, and I thought that rather sad, because my opening prayer always conveyed that I hoped councillors would listen to each other's viewpoints and learn to work in harmony for the good of the community they represented.

Besides the monthly council meetings there were other special events in which I had to play a part. Prime among these was the November Armistice Day service, held in the open air at the war memorial in front of the council offices. I asked Clive if there were any pointers he might like to give me concerning the service. What form would it take? Would there be any music? Any public singing? Filling me in on the details, he added, 'Your second in command will be a Catholic priest.'

'Oh,' I said, smiling a little to myself. 'I wonder how he'll take to that...'

'There'll also be a Methodist minister under your jurisdiction,' he went on. I saw that it would be an interesting reversal of more traditional roles.

The day dawned surprisingly dry and bright for November, and I walked in procession with the mayor, deputy mayor and members of the council, all in their official robes, to the place where the service was to be held. For my own part, I wore a simple dark suit, my minister's badge, and the SNU president's badge which had belonged to Gordon Higginson, for Spiritualist ministers have no special robes or other attire.

As we approached the microphones which had been set up, I noticed how very many people were gathered – a few thousand at least. Many high-ranking officers from the Army, Navy and Air Force were present, the latter group catching my eye because of my former association with the RAF.

I conducted the service in memory of those who had lost their physical lives in service to their country, emphasising in prayers, readings and hymns our duty to honour and respect their sacrifice. Afterwards, we processed back inside the council offices. During the refreshments that followed, a number of people came up to me and congratulated me, saying that they thought the service had gone very well and the words I had spoken were to the point and meaningful. Some noticed that I had not used a book to conduct the service and I told them it was not our practice to follow a set form of words – rather, we spoke from the heart.

As I stood sipping my tea, an Air-Vice Marshal approached me. We chatted for a while and he told me how much he had enjoyed the service. He asked if I had been in the forces myself and what rank I had held, and I replied that I had actually only been an AC2. Rather than cocking a snook at me he was quite friendly and asked what my religion was. I told him I was a Spiritualist. 'Oh, that's interesting,' he said, and sounded as if he meant it. I was also approached by another officer who had attended some of the other functions I'd been to. He was most complimentary about the service, and I later learned that he had become the vice-chancellor of Birmingham University.

I had wondered beforehand if there would be a degree of hostility towards me from the other religious ministers who took part in the service, but I can honestly say that I didn't notice any. Whether they had reservations, I don't know, but if they did, they certainly kept them to themselves.

Towards the end of Clive's mayoralty, in March 2002, I received a letter inviting me to the mayor's official ball. I would play a small part in the proceedings by saying a prayer before the meal. Other than that, Heather and I would be free to enjoy ourselves along with the other guests. As it turned out, we were seated next to the same RAF officer I had met at the Armistice Day Service, Air-Vice Marshal Tony Mason and his wife, with whom we had most interesting conversations.

All things considered it was quite a function, with many dignitaries present, and we really enjoyed ourselves. We had decided to stay overnight because I didn't want to drive all the way back to Stourbridge at midnight, particularly since I knew that I would probably enjoy a glass or two of wine during the evening. Arriving at our hotel after the ball, I discovered that a Spiritualist friend of ours had already visited to pay the bill – an act of generosity I have never forgotten.

My final duty as mayoral chaplain was on the day Clive stood down and a new mayor was inaugurated. Again, there was a procession, accompanied by the sound of trumpets, as we walked down onto the stage of a packed Town Hall and the ceremony commenced. My function, as always, was to open in prayer, and in doing so I made reference to 'the Great Spirit whom we call God'. It crossed my mind that someone of more orthodox sensibilities might take exception to this, but no one said a word afterwards. The ceremony proceeded, the new mayor was installed, and as the event drew to a close, so did my duties as chaplain.

A number of folk came to chat with me afterwards, all in a most amicable and appreciative way. Some were kind enough to say they had been quite inspired by the fact that I had carried out my duties in what they described as 'a dignified manner' and had not been 'bombastic' in the process. I thought that was nice of them. One commented wryly, 'Thank God you didn't draw it out like some we've had in the past!' This pleased me, since I had occasionally wondered if my prayers had been too short, and now I knew they had not!

At the end of the afternoon, Clive thanked me profusely for the way I had carried out my role as his chaplain, and I in turn thanked him for the opportunity he had given me.

To the best of my knowledge there has not been a Spiritualist mayoral chaplain before or since that time. It was a privilege for me, and a unique opportunity to fly a gentle flag for Spiritualism in a wholly unexpected way.

* * * *

The level of acceptance accorded to me as Spiritualist chaplain to the mayor of a prominent borough was a far cry from the way in which Spiritualists had been treated in former times. Though members of the public had thronged to demonstrations of mediumship during the Second World War, those mediums were still subject to considerable injustice under the law. Astonishingly, sections of the Vagrancy Act of 1824 could be invoked against them, classing them with persons such as

A woman deserting her bastard child

A person in a public place exposing indecent prints or exhibitions

A person lewdly and obscenely in a public place exposing his person with intent to insult a female

A male person who lives on the proceeds of prostitution or in a public place importunes for immoral purposes

Fortune tellers and mediums

You will see very clearly from this list the great injustice which was levelled at Spiritualist mediums, using just a few aspects of the law as it stood prior to the passing of the Fraudulent Mediums Act in 1951. There were many other legal anomalies, including provisions of the Witchcraft Act, which were unbelievably biased against genuine mediums.

In an attempt to address these blatant injustices, a deputation representing all Spiritualists met with representatives of the Home Office in 1943. Their purpose was to present the case for the removal of various provisions of the Vagrancy Act. This presentation by learned and respected Spiritualists was ultimately unsuccessful, it being stated by the Home Office that during the time of war it would be difficult to introduce legislation to amend Section 4 of the Vagrancy Act.

It would, however, be remiss of me if I did not recognise and record thanks to the members of that deputation, led by the great advocate for Spiritualism, Air Chief Marshal Lord Dowding.

His fellow deputation members were

S.J. Peters MA, LLD, MP

T.J. Brooks MBE, MP

A.E. Radford MP

G.E. Loseby (MP 1918-1922) Barrister at Law

A.H.L. Vigurs - President, Spiritualists' National Union

J.M. Stewart - Past President

J.B. McIndoe – Treasurer and Past President

A.J. Raffill – Vice-President

E.A. Keeling – General Secretary

G.A. Elkin - Solicitor

By 1951 the tide had turned, and we Spiritualists were ecstatic at the passing into law of the Fraudulent Mediums Act, together with the repeal of a number of sections of the Vagrancy and Witchcraft Acts, parts of which had until then most unjustly pertained to matters of mediumship. As a result of the passing of the new Act, we Spiritualists could now worship, and our mediums demonstrate their gift of communication with the next world, without fear of prosecution.

This momentous event came about through the generosity of a gentleman named Walter Munslow MP, who had been fortunate enough to win a ballot at the commencement of a new parliamentary session in November 1950. This gave him the right to put a Private Member's Bill before Parliament.

Walter Munslow was a practising Methodist, and a close friend of Tom Brooks, Member of Parliament for Castleford in Yorkshire and a dedicated Spiritualist. Walter admired Tom for his loyal service to Spiritualism and knew that his greatest desire was to promote a Bill which would give Spiritualists freedom. As a result, Walter chose to give up his own right to present a Bill and instead dedicated himself to assisting Tom in the preparation of what would become the Fraudulent Mediums Act which, incidentally, went through committee stages and two readings in the House of Commons without a single objection. What a generous gesture it was from Walter Munslow, who may never have known in this life the full significance of his kindness. I was fortunate enough to shake the hand of both these gentlemen at a later celebration rally.

* * * *

Like many of her mediumistic colleagues, Doris Collins was a fortunate beneficiary of the new legislation. From my earliest days of meeting her when she came to serve the church at Stourbridge, I had a degree of friendship with her. On other occasions when Heather and I would go down to London and join the merry throng of guests at the annual dinner of *Psychic News*, or attend various events at different venues, we would often bump into each other and she would always be friendly to us.

I was conscious, though, that over the years she had developed quite an ego, and the situation was amply illustrated when the annual Spiritualist of the Year award was announced. Instead of being its sole recipient, Doris had to share the award with an equally prominent medium, Doris Fisher Stokes. I suspected this decision was down to the wisdom of the editor, Maurice Barbanell – known to many as

'Barbie' – because, had he given the award solely to one or the other, there would undoubtedly have been an outbreak of hostilities. He was a clever man!

In consequence of that award, Doris's fame had grown, and she was in increasing demand, not only for her evidential mediumship but for her ability as a healer which, I was given to understand from those to whom she had given healing, was considerable, and was combined with a good deal of kindness.

Doris Collins

Her ability as a clairvoyant and clairaudient had developed steadily over the years and was very proficient, and from time to time she would give private sittings to well-known celebrities, including Peter Sellers, Frankie Howerd and Michael Bentine, to name just three. I felt, though, that to some extent she had rested upon her laurels by confining her work to the south of the country, particularly London, or going abroad to Switzerland and other parts of the European continent, as well as to South Africa and the USA.

By this time she had married her second husband, Philip McCaffrey, and though she had a capable manager, Larry O'Leary, it seemed that Philip had to all intents and purposes become her unofficial PR person. He was always saying 'Doris this...' or 'Doris that...' and seemed almost lost in her shadow.

It was around this time that the Arthur Findlay College at Stansted was struggling to attract people to its courses and events, and Robert Hartrick, then the chairman, talked with me about who we might book in order to draw more folk in. Almost all the lecturers, tutors and demonstrators were SNU people, and while Doris had been very closely associated with a SNU church in Woodford, East London, she had a high profile and made quite an impression wherever she went. So I said to Robert, 'Why don't we get Doris Collins in?' He replied that it was most unlikely she would come, but I suspected otherwise and asked him if he would like me to approach her. I did so, and she was delighted. There was no doubt about it – she attracted a lot of people during the days and weeks she spent at Stansted, especially Open Week, to which she came regularly from that point onward. True, some people had reservations about her style, because she was flamboyant and was a very big woman – you couldn't miss her physical presence – but she did a good job.

A few years earlier I had formed a friendship with Michaela Dennis, who with her first husband Armand was well known, having filmed and presented many scientific television programmes about animals. Some time after Armand's death, Michaela met and married a titled gentleman and in consequence became known as Lady Michaela Dennis. I always found her to be a very nice person, and in consequence asked her if she would come to Open Week, an invitation she readily accepted. Of course, when she and Doris were there at the same time, Doris always made a great display of it, but I believe they did develop quite a genuine friendship. Nevertheless, Doris always made sure she was there when the photographers were about!

For quite a few years Doris would take part in our annual Stourbridge weeks at the college and Philip would accompany her. It was a tradition that we would always have a trip out to some place or other on the Thursday afternoon, which our folk enjoyed. Over time I had begun to sense that Philip was a little disgruntled with the fact that he so often had to play second fiddle to Doris, for he was a successful person in his own right, having made quite a bit of money as a broker.

So it was that a day or two before our coach trips Philip would take Heather to one side and have a quiet word with her, asking if she would arrange some private sittings for

Doris so that he could come with us on the coach and leave her behind. He was wicked! He did this three years in a row, and I clearly remember that when we boarded the coach for Cambridge one year and people asked him where Doris was, he said a bit too cheerfully, 'Oh, she's all right, don't worry about her.' He liked to have us to himself!

On another occasion Doris and Philip stayed at a hotel in Clent, a few miles from Stourbridge, so that Doris could serve our church. I shepherded them to and fro when necessary and they seemed happy. But when I went to the hotel a few days later to pay the bill, the proprietor remarked with typically blunt Black Country humour, 'Oh they were nice people, but she's got a bit of an opinion of herself, hasn't she!'

In 2002, as Doris's health began to decline, Philip came more to prominence because she needed his help. Whether it was out of love or simply a sense of duty, I do not know, but it has to be said that he was very caring towards her. Eventually, she needed professional care and went into a nursing home.

I travelled to Milton Keynes to see her on a number of occasions, and when eventually she passed in September 2003, Philip came to Stourbridge to see us. He made no bones about it, telling us, 'I'm happier now than I've been for years.' Evidently their later years together had not been entirely happy.

'Eric,' he said. 'You and Heather have been so very kind to us and I want you to come out to Switzerland with me and stay at the hotel Doris and I always visited.' I don't know why he felt we had been kind, but perhaps it had something to do with the fact that I had achieved formal recognition for Doris by getting her a SNU diploma. She was an excellent demonstrator and deserved it. Philip had also expressed to me his feeling that Doris's very lengthy service as a medium had been completely overlooked, and so I had arranged for her to be presented with the SNU's Long Service Award.

A while later Heather and I were returning from Stansted and stopped off in Milton Keynes to visit Philip. He and Doris had a lovely bungalow with all kinds of very nice furniture, and the many awards Doris had received for this, that and the other were displayed on the walls. He had several times repeated his earlier invitation to accompany him to Switzerland and eventually we had agreed to go. But when he opened the door to us we were shocked. He looked so very, very ill and told us he was suffering from cancer.

I said to him, 'Philip – you mustn't go to Switzerland. You must stay here and have treatment.'

'Oh no,' he said. 'It's all booked up.' He was adamant about leaving the next day and wanted us to fly out and join him two or three days later. His nephew was going to drive him to the airport, he told us. 'Come into the bedroom,' he said. We followed him in and saw that his suitcase was on the bed, packed full. Our concern must have been evident, for he tried to reassure us, saying, 'Don't worry, I haven't got to do anything. Everything is ready. I'm going tomorrow and I want you to come out.' So he flew off to Switzerland the next day and we followed a couple of days later.

It was a nice hotel – quite small, and the two owners made us very welcome. They also delivered the sad but not unexpected news that Philip had been taken into hospital. The manager, a friend of Philip's, immediately drove us there and we found him in a beautiful private room overlooking the countryside. It was obvious that he was in a very serious condition, and the doctor indicated to us that he was unlikely to be around for very long. His nephew Paul arrived the next day and after a frank conversation with the medical team was told that Philip could go in a matter of a day or two. Two or three days later, he passed.

Paul wanted an orthodox Catholic funeral for his uncle and told me that he would make all the necessary arrangements. This was a delicate situation, and presented me with a problem, for I had conducted Doris's funeral and Philip had asked me in the presence of others if I would conduct his own when the time came. I had given him my assurance that I would.

In the end I had no alternative but to leave things to Paul, and a compromise was eventually achieved. I conducted the service and Paul invited Catholic representatives to play a part in it. These included a nun who spoke warmly about Philip. If I am not much mistaken, I believe he may have been generous to the Catholic church at earlier times in his life.

* * * *

By this time I had recovered well from my heart problems and my health was no longer the serious issue it had been. Nevertheless, I paid attention to the advice of friends and family that I should not push myself so hard and although Heather and I did not exactly put our feet up, we were able to enjoy life at a slightly more leisurely pace than in previous decades.

We remained as closely involved as we had ever been with the running of Stourbridge church and I continued to conduct a number of funerals, weddings and babies' naming services, at which I have always used a flower, as opposed to the water traditionally employed in orthodox baptism. As always, we participated in and helped with the organisation of several study weeks at the Arthur Findlay College, including Stourbridge, J.V. Trust and Highland weeks, and fulfilled a number of speaking engagements at churches in various parts of the UK. I also took an active part in college Open Weeks and attended meetings of the AFC committee, of which I was chairman for many years and have been a member since 1971.

In 2003 I had the honour of being involved in the rededication of the Sanctuary at the college, since the J.V. Trust had contributed a sizeable sum of money to its enhancement. This included a new internal roof structure, the repainting in gold of the wrought iron braces, an entirely new lighting system, plus new raked seating, platform and carpeting. A great deal of this work was carried out during the annual volunteers' week under the direction of the then president Duncan Gascoyne.

Later that year Heather and I travelled to Holland in the company of mediums Eileen Davies and Len Lobban to fulfil a long-standing invitation from Dutch Spiritualists Dick and Willemyn Bessam and their family. We were guests at their home in The Hague, which was a special experience, for their large house was a buzzing centre of spiritual research and activity. Eileen, Heather and Len gave demonstrations of spirit communication, and I gave talks and lectures. One particular event in which we jointly took part was held in a large hall within a memorial park and proved to be very successful for all four of us.

The following May, Heather and I were once again involved in Open Week, she as usual organising more than thirty mediums to give private interviews – a mammoth task. Shortly afterwards we travelled to the Oxfordshire home of Denzil Fairbairn, nephew of the famous physical medium Jack Webber, who passed to spirit in 1940. We had been invited to attend a physical séance with the medium David Thompson and saw it as an important opportunity to further our lifelong research and investigation into the various forms of mediumship. In addition to witnessing rare physical phenomena, we were impressed by the verified spirit contacts made with various recipients who were present.

Chapter 15

On psychical research and experiments

I have written elsewhere in this book of the importance I attach to thorough and properly conducted psychical research. There is perhaps a perception among some people that Spiritualists are well-meaning but slightly gullible folk who will sit around in dark rooms and accept almost anything that is said or done. This is, or should be, far from the truth.

Throughout my life in Spiritualism I have always been at pains to verify information given to me through mediums, even those who have been well known to me personally. It is vitally important that communications purporting to come from the spirit world should be treated objectively, and their veracity established.

In addition, where physical mediumship is concerned, the resulting manifestations can sometimes be so dramatic as to seem beyond belief. If the credibility of such mediumship is to be assured, it is therefore vitally important that controls are put in place to ensure that the medium – or indeed others in the séance room – could not possibly be responsible for any phenomena which occur. I have already described in chapter four the elaborate precautions that were taken to ensure the integrity of an Alec Harris materialisation séance I attended in the late 1940s. Mr Harris's séances were conducted in a good degree of light, but the need for proper controls is even more vital when, as is often the case today, the proceedings take place in almost total darkness.

Throughout the history of Spiritualism there have been many who have carried out meticulous research into mediumship and psychic faculties of all kinds – clairvoyance and clairaudience, trance, independent direct voice, materialisation, physical phenomena – and some of those researchers have been distinguished individuals, to say the least. The great physicist Sir Oliver Lodge, the chemist and physicist Sir William Crookes, the French physiologist Dr Charles Richet, Baron Albert von Schrenck Notzing and the classicist Frederic Myers, to name but a few, devoted major parts of their lives to establishing the genuineness or otherwise of phenomena which could not be explained by known material laws. Today, it seems that far less research is taking place, but nonetheless there are a number of respected persons such as psychologists Professor David Fontana and Dr Alan Gauld, and the astronomer Professor Archie Roy, who devote significant time and effort to furthering the cause of psychical studies and publishing detailed accounts of their work.

I was a great admirer of Maurice Barbanell, editor of *Psychic News* and *Two Worlds,* and an excellent journalist. Another journalist whom I knew to a lesser degree, but for whom I had a lot of time, was Ernest Thompson. Ernest held a fellowship from the SNU and wrote many of its early educational papers.

At one point in his career he was the publisher and editor of *Psychic Realm*, which he subtitled 'The voice of progressive Spiritualism'. He wrote books under his own name and also under the pseudonym Mark Dyne.

He was the originator of the Spirit Electronic Society, based in Manchester, where he conducted experiments in communication methods using the application of what he called 'electro-psychic energy'. Other prominent and respected members of the Society, including Captain Ernest Gill and Dr Karl Muller, confirmed the very favourable results that were obtained with this method in heightening the sensitivity of the subject.

Ernest Thompson also had an association with the Delaware Laboratory in Oxford and a group in Holland. They were working on projects which, like his, were producing interesting results. Sadly, I lost touch with Ernest before he passed and am now unsure what eventually happened to those groups, which all conducted experiments with trance under strict test conditions.

Before using his 'electro-psychic energy' equipment – an electrical coil with contacts which could be attached to the medium's body – to assist in the trance condition, he would begin by asking whether the subject had been in trance before and, if so, whether it was a regular occurrence, and how many others sat with the subject at the time.

He would take the subject's pulse, make a note of it, and once they had gone into trance, would take it again, first asking permission of the spirit control. He would then compare the two, on most occasions finding a considerable difference between them. He would also seek the controlling entity's permission to ask questions, in an attempt to eliminate self-delusion as a possible source of the apparent trance condition.

Another technique was to determine the difference between the positive and negative energies from the circuitry and the medium. This was very interesting to note, the latter usually being negative during the trance state.

How I wish some of those conditions were applied today, when almost every student wishes to be, or thinks they are, a trance medium. I hope I am not being over critical when I say that so many of them suffer from self-delusion and need to be acquainted with the fact.

There are also in the movement as a whole some teachers who are promoting trance all too readily and quickly. Their behaviour does no good for our image and reflects badly upon good, genuine trance mediumship.

Whilst speaking about communicative work, I have doubts and reservations about the methods which some of our exponents adopt during public demonstrations, particularly the 'throwing out' of snippets of information to the congregation or audience in the hope that they will apply to someone. In fairness, the information may well fit and be meaningful to somebody, and may well be expanded to something more evidential, but analysis carried out by me, and to a much more systematic extent by serious researchers, indicates that approximately sixty per cent of early 'throw-out' details could apply to a high percentage of the people present.

I do urge our demonstrators to make every effort to go direct to the recipient, or at least to the approximate location where they believe the message applies. This will make all the difference to the quality of the communication, as well as enabling an easier inter-flow from the communicating spirit. You may say it is easy for me to criticise, since I am not a medium as such, but I am very much aware of the various degrees of sensitivity and my comments are based on the excellence of medium friends of mine who have sat in circles to perfect their gifts in that way.

Speaking of gifts, I am sad to learn that some of our teachers maintain that mediumship is not necessarily a gift and can be learned by almost anyone. I cannot subscribe to that view, for my long experience shows that mediumship, as opposed to psychism, is a privileged gift and should be carefully nurtured by those who have been granted it. Harold Vigurs, a former president of the SNU, shared this opinion, as did the researcher and writer Brigadier Roy Firebrace, and of course, Maurice Barbanell.

Incidentally, each of them pleaded for more research into what lay behind the whole business of communication. After Harold's passing I had a most detailed and convincing form of communication from him, the most striking aspect of it being that he found things in his new world very different from what he had imagined them to be while still in the body. He added that Gordon Higginson, whom he had met in that new world, shared the same view. Doesn't that tend to suggest that learning, knowledge and experience, of which we may have much, would seem to reveal but a fraction of what life in the astral sphere is like – the full reality being beyond our comprehension? Recognising that should not deter us in our search. Rather it should act as a stimulus.

I have known my fellow Spiritualist Geoff Griffiths for over fifty years, and he recently reminded me of the occasion of our first meeting. It took place in the early 1950s at the annual South Wales summer school in Penarth. Geoff and I proceeded to reminisce about the people we had the privilege of meeting, and agreed how fortunate we had been to encounter so many luminaries of the Spiritualist movement at that time. The school attracted people not only from the UK but from many other countries, each of whom played an active role in research and investigation.

One such person was Madame Simone St. Clair of France, who had been awarded her country's highest honour for the heroic part she played in the resistance movement during the German occupation of her country. Another lady, who had also been recognised for her resistance to the occupation, was Madame Van Sarne of Holland. By virtue of their experiences and research, both these women had become convinced of life's continuity after death.

Geoff also recalled an experiment which took place at Penarth's Paget Rooms, in which we both played a part, helping to build a cabinet on the large stage there, so that Gordon Higginson's abilities as a physical medium could be tested.

One hundred and thirty-five people were present, seated in rows, and all were in a position to see whatever might take place. Controls were in place to ensure that there could be no possibility of fraud, the sitters on either side of Gordon holding his hands throughout the duration of the séance.

After being searched by four men, Gordon was permitted to enter the cabinet. There followed a period of singing of a wide range of songs, and as was the custom in Wales, it raised the roof. It was not too long before knocks and raps were heard, and they were not emanating from the assembled crowd. Then everybody observed the two séance trumpets – marked with luminous bands – rise and dance around, sometimes high above our heads.

After a while this activity ceased, and was followed by a period of silence. The guides then permitted the red light to be switched on. Our eyes having become accustomed to it, it was sufficiently bright to enable everyone to see what might manifest.

Gradually, streams of ectoplasm began to flow from Gordon's mouth, extending several feet from his body. People watched amazed as, little by little, some of this took on the form of the head and shoulders of a person, which was recognised by one of those present as being that of a deceased relative.

The whole experience lasted over an hour, at the close of which Gordon returned to his normal state and was given a glass of water. Those of us who witnessed this remarkable display of spirit power were left in awe, since a phenomenon of this type, shown to such a large number of people simultaneously, was unknown if not unique.

As a complete contrast to other forms of his mediumship, I persuaded Gordon on another occasion to use his skill in a form of billet reading with a variety of sealed objects. The results were spectacular and raised many questions concerning the nature of energy fields, which are not clearly understood. Similar types of experiment were attempted with Robin Stevens, Gerard Smith, Sally Ferguson and Stephen O'Brien, all with different degrees of success.

Some of my early experiences in mediumship were through the avenue of psychometry, when the medium would hold an object which had been worn or frequently handled by the sitter. The medium would relay impressions he or she sensed from the object. Of course this raised the question of whether inanimate things have an energy of their own, a theory that has been accepted by some researchers, particularly where ancient objects are concerned.

On occasions, these psychometric impressions would contain information relating to a person who had died. Whilst this in itself was to some degree proof of survival, it rarely stood up to close analysis, for the simple reason that many a good psychic can be fairly adept at this technique, though they may not actually be a medium. A capable psychic can pick up many things from living people and from objects, whereas a medium's primary purpose is to prove survival of the human spirit by connecting with those who have passed on to the next phase of existence.

In 1968 I was instrumental in forming a secular research group which became known as the Stourbridge Society for Psychical and Allied Studies. My intention was to conduct non-denominational research and encourage others to explore a whole range of subjects outside the norm. Amongst our members were a former Baptist minister, the deputy editor of our local paper, named Dennis Elwell, and a scientist living in Stourbridge. Percy Wilson and Maurice Barbanell thought the society a good idea, and paid tribute to it in print more than once.

We held regular meetings in the local junior library, often attracting a hundred or so people, many of them quite young. We invited a variety of specialist speakers and mediums, and also some who could demonstrate their areas of research, including an acupuncturist, a hypnotist and an astrologer. When mediums were invited, we laid down strict conditions and controls.

One who came to speak to us was the dowser Cecil Mabey, author of several books on his subject. He agreed to set up a demonstration at Kinver Edge, a local beauty spot. A few days beforehand I made it my business to go along to the water board and ask if I could have a plan of the water courses and pipes. They were very suspicious about why I wanted it, and called a more senior staff member to come and speak to me. I told him about the society and about Cecil Mabey's dowsing and he eventually conceded the point, giving me the plans. He also gave me information about various related things.

On the appointed day we gathered at Kinver, but instead of getting on with his demonstration, Cecil embarked on a rather long-winded talk about dowsing. I could see that people were almost dozing off, so I told him that I thought it was going to rain any minute. 'Oh,' said Cecil, 'I'd better get on with it then!'

Grasping his hazel-wood dowsing rods, he walked in this direction and that, stopping from time to time to tell us in detail about the depth of the water beneath and the direction in which it was flowing. He never saw the plans I had from the water board, but when Dennis and I checked them afterwards, we found that everything Cecil had said was one hundred per cent accurate.

We never used hymns or music at those SSPAS meetings in the library, as generally happens at Spiritualist churches and séances, yet those who were mediumistically sensitive were nonetheless able to produce very good proof of survival. That being so, it caused me to wonder if, in always using music or prayers, we Spiritualists may have fallen into a routine which restricts us. For instance, just take the fact that most of our physical work nowadays is done in the dark, whereas events that have taken place in the relatively recent past prove beyond doubt that physical phenomena and even full materialisations are perfectly possible in lighted conditions. Experiences enjoyed in Rhodesia (now Zimbabwe) by mediums Albert Best and Stuart Lawson will serve to illustrate this point.

Albert, a highly respected clairvoyant and clairaudient medium, had lost his wife and children during the Second World War. Decades later, while demonstrating his mediumship on tour in Rhodesia, he was taken on one of his free days to a small village which was home to a local 'Medicine Man'. It was the middle of the day and the African sun shone down.

Greeting Albert, the Medicine Man surprised him by saying that he had been waiting for him. The two men sat down quietly together and after a while the Medicine Man slowly raised his arm. Underneath it were the miniature materialised forms of Albert's wife and children.

Some time later, Stuart Lawson was in the same area and, having heard of Albert's experience, decided to pay his own visit to the Medicine Man. Again, the arm was raised, and in the bright African daylight Stuart was able to see a loved one again.

I therefore wonder whether it is the case that we in the western world have conditioned ourselves to believe that we have to abide by certain practices, and have by our own minds limited in some ways the manifestation of the spirit people into our physical world. We seem almost too fixated on having darkness in the physical séance room, or, at best, the very faintest red light, yet the Swedish physical medium Einer Nielsen did have good phenomena take place in relatively bright red light.

Regarding clairvoyance and clairaudience, I was inclined to the view that we should perhaps experiment with controls such as blindfolding mediums so that they had no opportunity to draw any visual indications from the person to whom they were giving evidence. I also favoured the additional control of having a proxy answer 'yes' or 'no' on the recipient's behalf, thus avoiding any unconscious clues being picked up from the tone of the recipient's own voice.

In 1969, during one of our Stourbridge weeks at Stansted Hall we proposed another rather unusual experiment with our principal demonstrators and lecturers – Gordon Higginson, Mary Duffy and Stephen O'Brien. Gordon was quite willing; Mary was slightly reluctant but agreed without any great hesitation; Stephen was most reluctant, perhaps because he was a young, up-and-coming medium

Stephen O'Brien

and had never done anything like it before. But I have persuasive ways and managed to convince all three to take part!

We conducted the experiment in the library, which we were using as a lecture room. Heather and I were present with the three mediums – no one else was there. Chairs were laid out in rows in readiness for the evening demonstration and I asked each medium to give a message to any empty chair they chose. We duly recorded those messages on tape.

In the evening, the students, having no knowledge of the experiment we had conducted, came into the library and sat down in whichever chair took their fancy. We then played the messages to the occupants of the designated chairs.

Despite his earlier anxiety and reservations, Stephen's efforts were reasonably successful; Mary's were much more successful. When it came to relaying Gordon's message, a gentleman was seated in the designated chair and the evidence he received was mind-blowing. Absolutely mind-blowing. The man was in tears at the contact he received from his wife, and the level of detail in it fascinated me. It concerned their marriage, their home, how his wife had passed and the words of love that he had written on a card and placed in her coffin.

We carried out similar experiments on a number of other occasions, notably when a medium named Robin Stevens was booked to serve Stourbridge church. I asked him whether he was prepared to take part and he agreed without too much reluctance. The plan was that he would sit at home and record his impressions before coming to the church (he lived the best part of a hundred miles away).

When he arrived during the late afternoon he more or less pinpointed where he wanted to place each message, but he hadn't been in a position to designate the precise area. At the back of the church we had a long bench-type seat and some members of the committee would almost always choose to sit there. I would sometimes say to them, 'You should learn to sit in different parts of the church and not hog that seat. Let other people sit on it.' I remember that one particular couple were quite fed up with me for that and said rather crossly, 'We'll sit where we like!' (I was much younger and less forceful in those days!)

Well, on the evening of Robin's visit they were sitting on the back row, leaving a designated chair empty. But just a moment or two before Robin started his demonstration, be damned if the lady didn't get up and go and sit in that chair! To put it mildly, she was flabbergasted by the information Robin gave her, and she was a bit of a hardened Spiritualist. So the experiment proved very successful and to his credit Robin asked if he could do one on another occasion. He later did a blindfolded demonstration and also a demonstration of billet reading, which few in England, besides Gordon Higginson, had done.

On other occasions I persuaded Robin Stevens, Gordon Higginson and Gerard Smith to be completely blindfolded and to demonstrate clairvoyance and clairaudience to the people assembled before them.

To ensure that the mediums could not see the congregation, or where any individual was sitting, each was blindfolded before being led into the library either by me or another member of the team. When the mediums chose to address a particular recipient, that person was not allowed to answer audibly – they merely nodded yes or no to another person who would respond on their behalf.

Gerard Smith

Apart from being very successful, the results of this experiment were intriguing, in that they offered an insight into the way mediumship could operate under such restrictive conditions. Since I

I ordain Mary Duffy as a minister of the SNU

believe that contacts are generally more rewarding and successful when the medium has the benefit of the vocal response of a recipient, to have a third person speaking is demanding. But in each case the mediums passed this test with flying colours.

On at least one other occasion we experimented with two mediums linking together on the same spirit contact. For instance, Mary Duffy would be drawn to a person in the room and, after relaying information about a communicating spirit, would hand over to Gerard Smith to relay whatever information he was receiving from the same entity. The routine would sometimes be reversed with a similar degree of success. It was amazing how accurately the evidence emerged from links such as these, on each occasion being confirmed by its recipient.

Of course, people might say that it should not be difficult for two mediums to operate in this way, but before dismissing the process as being easy, they should remember that each medium's sensitivity works in a different way from any other's and as such is unique.

On another occasion, Jill Harland was asked to sit in an upstairs room at the Arthur Findlay College, having been

Jill Harland

given no access to the downstairs lecture room in which the audience had gathered.

The idea was for her to 'tune in' with her sensitivity, then, as she was inspired, write down on a card the name of a piece of music. Each card was placed face-down on a tray and covered with a cloth, prior to being carried downstairs. Heather, waiting in the lecture room, would then be offered the tray by a student so that she had no contact with the cards. She would draw out a card, still face down, and use her sensitivity to pick out the person for whom she felt the card was intended. That person would then turn over the card to reveal the title which, in the majority of cases, proved to be meaningful in terms of the music and/or the title. Jill, who had been a well-known professional singer, would then sing the song, which often brought tears of joy to the person whose card it was.

Our own home was no stranger to psychical research. In addition to holding a regular circle with two friends, Harry and Marjorie Saitch, at which a great deal of survival evidence was obtained, we also conducted simple experiments to test the psychic ability of our dog, a much-loved Alsatian named Yana.

In our loft we had an old scarecrow that had been used for a Bonfire Night supper at church. With Yana in the garden we moved it down into the lounge and placed it in an area where we believed we had witnessed Yana sensing things in the past. When we called her in from the garden, she went up to the scarecrow and sniffed it a little but had no real interest in it.

She showed none of the signs she had previously exhibited in that part of the room and did not even prick up her ears.

On other occasions we prepared two cards, each bearing a single word. One read 'Bert' and the other, 'Pop'. Neither of these men had ever visited the house in physical life. We then selected just one card and concentrated our thoughts on the particular name written on it. We were very much surprised by Yana's agitation as she paused for some considerable time in front of the card.

Another unusual incident not only surprised me but proved to me that there is certainly more than one way in which those on the 'other side' can communicate their continuing existence in a world near to our own, along with their earthly memories which are so precious to their loved ones still living on earth.

In January 1980 I conducted a funeral service at Birmingham's Perry Barr crematorium for a lady named Nan Evans. The crematorium was packed, and the congregation included many black friends. Mrs Evans' husband was a sick man and had been allowed to leave his hospital bed to attend her funeral. Ten days later he passed, and I conducted his funeral in the same place. Their daughters – Paula and Olga – wrote to thank me for the 'sensitive services' I had carried out.

Shortly after the second funeral I was surprised to receive a letter from my old friend, Albert Best, who had just returned from South Africa to his home in Glasgow. The letter contained the extraordinary information that whilst in South Africa he had suddenly heard a voice saying to him, 'Thank Eric for the wonderful send-offs for me and my Nan in Perry Barr.'

Albert Best

The voice then added, 'Ask Eric to give our love to Paula and Olga and tell them we are near to them often.'

This was exceptionally fine evidence, since Albert had never once met, or even heard of, Mr and Mrs Evans. They were sincere and hard-working members of a church in Lacells, Birmingham, which had a fair number of West Indian members in the congregation. After his wife's passing, Mr Evans frequently said that his one desire was to be reunited with her, for they had been a very devoted couple. The communication received by Albert Best in South Africa, concerning events which had taken place so many thousands of miles away, clearly illustrated that distance is no object to those in the spirit world.

In subsequent years I have tried, when possible, to continue with experiments in mediumship, the most recent taking place at the Arthur Findlay College during Senior Citizens' week in June 2010. The editor of *Psychic News* was present, and the following week the newspaper carried her account of the experiment, which also included a medium's-eye view of the importance of experimentation in the ongoing process of development. This is what she wrote:

Three mediums, three ladies' scarves and the power of the spirit have combined to yield impressive survival evidence in an experimental demonstration at Stansted Hall.

Mediums John Conway, Jill Harland and Gerard Smith were willing and good-natured participants in an experiment devised by SNU Honorary President Minister Eric Hatton during Senior Citizens' Week, an annual event administered by the SNU's Fund of Benevolence.

As the mediums remained well out of the way in another part of the Arthur Findlay College, the 60-strong audience assembled in the Lecture Room, each taking whichever seat they wanted.

Five minutes before the start of the demonstration Eric Hatton took to the platform and explained that the mediums would work blindfolded, making it impossible for them to see where people were sitting or to pick up any other visual clues. In addition, audience members were told not to answer if one of the mediums came to them with a message. Instead they were asked to shake or nod their head as appropriate so that the person sitting next to them would speak to the medium on their behalf, depriving the mediums of any aural input from recipients.

Three volunteers were then invited to go to the medium's room, blindfold the demonstrators and lead them into the Lecture Room. This was to be done in silence.

One by one the mediums were led through the room and up onto the platform – a steep step for anyone deprived of the faculty of sight, and necessitating a good deal of trust in those who were doing the guiding! All three mediums safely in their seats, the demonstration began with a message through Gerard Smith. All details were accepted without hesitation. John Conway and Jill Harland delivered messages to two further sitters – again accepted as correct.

All continued to go well until John Conway embarked on another message which, he said, was for someone sitting in the second row on the left hand side of the room. He followed up with detailed references to the Welsh mining town of Aberfan, where in 1966 a disaster had taken place, killing many. John added that the person receiving the message should also know of a child who had died as a result of the events there. This information was met with total silence – no one in the second row could understand it.

Chairing the demonstration, Eric Hatton suggested that perhaps someone in the rows immediately in front or behind might be able to accept what had been offered.

Again, silence. On the platform John was clearly puzzled, since throughout the evening his information had met with a constant 'Yes'.

'This evidence just wasn't hitting the mark,' John told PN. 'Then, all of a sudden one of my inspirers – Thomas – told me about an empty chair, so I asked the audience if there was an empty chair in the second row and they answered that there was.'

John then asked if the chair had been reserved for someone and was told that it had not. It then emerged that the empty chair had been occupied by the same person for several previous events during the week, but on this particularly evening she had come in at the last moment and was sitting at the back of the room. Indicating to the person sitting next to her that she could accept everything John had said concerning Aberfan, he spoke up on her behalf and the evidence at last found its home.

'It goes to prove the power of the spirit,' said John. 'The mechanics really interest me. It's as if everything has already been planned.'

I asked John how he had felt about being blindfolded for such a long period, and whether he thought such experiments with mediumship were important.

'It was a bit disorienting at first,' he told me. 'But the loss of the physical sense heightens your awareness of the vibrations in the room.

'I think experiments are the way forward. There can be no progress in our mediumship if things remain static. Experiments are a test of mediumship, strengthening and developing it. Without that, mediums can get stuck on a plateau. They have to push themselves forward.'

* * * *

I regard it as very unfortunate that so little scientific work has been done in recent decades, and I wonder whether the current lack of long-term research into mediumship is ultimately down to the mediums or the researchers. When I think of the mediums of days gone by, I am rather disposed to think that they were somewhat more dedicated than many today. Eileen Garrett, for example, was committed to understanding the workings of her remarkable mediumship, almost begging researchers to study her and shed light upon her work. The great trance mediums Gladys Osborne Leonard and Leonora Piper were studied over decades, teaching us much about the subtleties of communication in general, and trance control in particular.

In saying that, I acknowledge that we do have many dedicated mediums, but few seem willing to submit themselves to scientific experimentation and research. Of course, some people will say that the case for spirit communication is already made, but there is no case that can't be enhanced, is there?

Chapter 16

Shared joys and deep sorrows

*Heather and her mediumship • Fifty years of togetherness •
After sorrow, new joy • Laura, my sister*

I have already mentioned that Heather's mother and father were both dedicated Spiritualists, and that she was brought up to regard the presence of spirit people as completely normal and natural. From childhood she was mediumistically sensitive, possessing a considerable gift.

Her occasional demonstrations were always conducted in a very gentle, quiet way – there was nothing forceful in the way she delivered messages or spoke to recipients. She also had one particular custom which gradually became known as her special 'trademark'. Whenever she demonstrated she would always have a handkerchief tucked into her bracelet. Gordon Higginson would sometimes pull her leg about it (and he wasn't the only one!) but she would take it in good part and we would all three laugh about it together.

While Heather demonstrated in a number of places over the years – Stansted Hall, Darlington, Blackpool, Norwich, Bournemouth, South Wales, Belfast, Scotland, and even abroad on rare occasions – I felt that in some ways it was sad that she would not go out and take services on a Sunday as so many mediums do. She just did not feel it was right to do so, and preferred to be in Stourbridge, supporting me and the church. I believe she did this at the cost of her own mediumship, of which many people spoke so highly. In essence, I feel that to some extent she sacrificed her gift for my sake. Though our children tell me they were never at a disadvantage I also reflect on the sacrifices they must have

*The platform party – Heather and myself
with Gordon after sharing a service*

made in their early years, for they were often minded by other people while Heather and I were away at Spiritualist meetings and events. Certainly we always tried to look after them and always showed them love.

When Heather gave private interviews, or sittings, as they are now more commonly known, she would always do them at the church – never at home. I don't remember her ever taking money for them – everything was done for the benefit of the church. One day, a lady we had never met before came for a sitting which had been booked in advance on her behalf. As was my habit, I went along to the church just as it was about to finish and within minutes the lady emerged from the small room where sittings take place. She said 'Hello' to me and I spoke with her, asking, 'How did you get on? Was the interview helpful to you?'

'I don't know how your wife does it,' she told me. 'It was so wonderfully helpful.' She added that she would like to acknowledge what she had received and would do her best to let other people know about it. Having never seen her before,

I asked her where she came from, and she replied that she lived just outside Malvern – a town some thirty miles from Stourbridge. We talked a little longer and I learned, among other things, that her name was Mrs Morgan. Shortly afterwards she went on her way, clearly grateful for what Heather had given her in the sitting. We subsequently discovered that she was in fact the wife of the owner of Morgan Cars, the firm which produces famous handmade English sports cars. Later, other people from that area came for sittings with Heather. Without exception they praised her and the help she had given them.

On one occasion, a chap arrived at the church for a sitting and we had no idea who he was. We learned afterwards that he had come because he was perplexed about his career, having suffered a number of disappointments, and was hoping to receive some guidance about whether or not he should continue with what he was doing. Later, he explained that he had received personal evidence of a high order, adding that Heather had told him his career would take on a new lease of life and he would be more successful than ever. His real name was Fitzgerald, but you may know him better as the popular singer Tony Christie.

On another occasion Heather and I were at the London Spiritual Mission, where Albert Best was due to demonstrate and I was to give an address. After the morning service, the three of us went upstairs to have lunch with Rosalind Cattanach, the Mission's resident secretary, and Albert asked us if, later that afternoon, we would go downstairs with him to the church library where he had something to do. He did not tell us what that something was, but we agreed without hesitation.

After lunch, Albert, Heather and I made our way downstairs to the church, and Albert asked if we would mind sitting in another room while he met with someone privately. A while later he called us in, obviously having given a private sitting to the lady who was in the room. Heather and I had no idea who she was, but Albert asked if we would join with him in giving her healing. We agreed, and were later told that it had been quite successful. The mystery sitter was Ruth, Lady Fermoy, quite a famous lady, being not only a Lady-in-Waiting to Queen Elizabeth, the Queen Mother, but also Princess Diana's grandmother.

As I reflect back over our married life, I realise just how much Heather contributed to the running of the church in Stourbridge. She was involved in almost all its activities and chaired many sub-committees. Even now, church members speak of how much they looked to her for guidance, as well as for contact with their 'dead' loved ones. Never did they ask in vain, for many have told me that her contribution to their lives at times of great need was their salvation.

As our golden wedding anniversary drew near, our family frequently raised the question of how we were going to celebrate it. Quite honestly, we were flummoxed, and just couldn't decide what to do. If we held a dinner or some other celebration for our wider family, we ran the risk of leaving out someone on the periphery and we didn't want to do that for fear of causing offence.

After much thought and discussion we decided that the best thing would be to have a celebration dinner at The Four

We celebrate our Golden Wedding
with Lisa and Jon

Stones, a very nice restaurant in Clent, for our children and grandchildren only. It took place on 28th December, the day after our official anniversary. The evening was especially meaningful to us because it was spent in the company of those we loved most – Lisa, Jon, Tristan, Alex, Jamie, Philippa and Fiona.

As a means of embracing other people in the celebrations, particularly those friends who in some ways had become almost as close to us as members of our family, we decided to invite them, along with others from the church and elsewhere for whom we had particular respect, to a dinner at the church.

We sent out invitations to 150 people but didn't tell them exactly what they were for – saying simply that they should come for 'a special evening'. Each and every one of them turned up on the night, to be met with the sight of a church that was decorated with large balloons and bunting. The tables were adorned by cloths of alternating colours and each had its own vase of fresh flowers. It made a splendid picture, festive and colourful. We gave our guests a slap-up meal, prepared by an excellent firm of outside caterers who served up a wide range of hot and cold food, all absolutely first class.

Our principal guests were my sister Laura and her husband Ray, who kept repeating how proud they were to be there. Our good friend Barry Smith and his wife were also guests that night, and Barry, an accomplished accordion player, gave us many moments of musical pleasure during the evening. The comedian Tommy Munden, a friend for more than sixty years, also came, and celebrated the event with a few good jokes!

Later, a number of people said they wished they could have come along, but realistically we had to restrict things in some way, otherwise we would have had four hundred or more turning up. I don't think there were any who took offence.

The memory of that joyous occasion, celebrating the incalculable blessing of fifty years' extremely happy marriage, is one I will always treasure, especially in light of the tragedy which was to strike just a few months later.

My long involvement with Spiritualism and psychical research has repeatedly shown me that when people lose a dearly loved one they are out of step with life, often for some considerable time. There are few who do not feel the hurt and anguish of loss, and in this age of declining religious influence people frequently struggle in vain to find answers to their vital questions concerning life and death. Even for those who are regular church goers, the answer does not always emerge from the inadequate conventional advice that one should have faith and read what the Bible has to say. Imagine, then, how much more difficult it must be for those who have no faith at all, and of course statistics show this to be a very large body of people in the United Kingdom.

When Heather passed into the next life in June 2007, I – even with all my experience and knowledge of life's continuity – felt numb and longed to hear from her – to know for myself that she was all right and had been met by loved ones who awaited her coming. I would be telling a lie if I said I had not yearned for proof of her survival.

Such was the strength and power of the bond of our intertwined lives that I felt deep within myself that she would do her utmost to take away my hurt and prove she was near. Through the excellent mediumship of Gerard Smith, Eileen Davies and John Conway, to name but three, I received graphic and detailed personal evidence which surprised even me. In some sittings with these three, reference was made by Heather to incidents which I had long forgotten, and to verify them I had to make searching enquiries to confirm the accuracy of the details. Some were extremely personal, and though I would love to share their veracity here, I cannot, because in doing so I would be betraying a pact that Heather and I made.

There have been other mediums who have conveyed meaningful messages to me from Heather and her family, and I have appreciated all of them, but Gerard, Eileen and John, each in their own humble way, provided me with evidence that was superb. Though they would not wish it, I cannot do other than shower praise upon them, with a multitude of thanks.

Since Heather's passing, those who knew and cared for her have often asked me why her heart condition was not diagnosed and in some way treated before she was admitted to Coventry University Hospital for such major surgery.

In fact, she had been diagnosed several years earlier with an irregular heartbeat, and this was treated with medication. Further tests, conducted eleven months prior to her operation, showed her also to have a faulty mitral valve, and her medication was altered to take account of that. Subsequent investigations over the next few months revealed that she also needed to undergo heart bypass surgery.

The advice we received from Dr Craig Scott Barr – the same cardiologist at Russells Hall Hospital who had treated me in 2001 – was of the highest order, and it was on this that we made the decision to allow cardiac surgeon Mr Ramesh Patel, apparently one of the most capable in the country, to carry out the surgery, which would also include a Cox Maze procedure to eliminate atrial fibrillation – a fast and erratic heartbeat.

Complicated and serious though it was, the surgery proved successful, and in the days immediately following it Heather made good progress. She was nursed in the intensive care unit, and it was only after she was transferred to an ordinary ward that problems started to manifest and her condition began to deteriorate. Tests showed that she had contracted a viral infection.

We had expected her to be home within ten to fourteen days of the operation, but five weeks later she was still in hospital and the deterioration in her health had become much more pronounced. I visited her twice a day throughout this period, taking her nourishing home-made soups and other items that might tempt her to eat, but I was becoming increasingly concerned by her condition.

Deeply worried, I asked Dr Barr to have her transferred to the nearer Russells Hall Hospital in Dudley, which he duly did. The care she was given there was excellent, but the damage had already been done. Special cultures were grown in an attempt to identify the precise nature of her infection, but alas, they were not effective.

Although she told me on several occasions prior to her passing that she was aware of the presence of family members and dear friends who had left this life, I tried to convince myself that they had only come to dispense healing to her. Even when, just a little while before she passed, she told me in detail of the spirit visitors who filled the room, I closed my eyes to the reality of what was happening.

Eleven weeks after the operation, Heather passed to the world of spirit. As I relive those moments three-and-a-half years later, I still cannot escape my feelings of loss and loneliness. Surrounded though I am by family and friends, and despite my involvement in so many activities, I long for our reunion.

I find it hard to forgive the hospital in Coventry for their lack of hygiene, for the surgery had been successful and a serious infection was something which could almost certainly have been avoided if proper precautions had been taken.

* * * *

In August 2007, just two months after Heather's passing, Jonathan and his fiancée Fiona went ahead with their wedding. As Heather lay in hospital she had been so pleased to hear about all the plans they had made.

The big day dawned bright and sunny, a particular blessing since it had been raining constantly during the preceding week, and the beautiful weather continued throughout the lovely day we all spent together.

Just outside Sutton Coldfield, in the district of Warmley, is a striking building named New Hall – a Tudor house surrounded by a rectangular moat and thought to be one of the oldest moat houses in Britain. Its Great Chamber was built to accommodate Henry VIII when he visited Sutton Coldfield, and it was there that Jon and Fiona exchanged their marriage vows.

Jon had paid me – his dad – the greatest of compliments by asking me to be his best man. Though it embarrasses me to say so, he told me that I was 'the best man' he knew, and I felt so honoured and proud at that.

Photographs of the newly-married couple, together with their four bridesmaids – Jon's daughters Alexandra, Philippa and Ella, and Fiona's daughter Mia, were taken inside the Hall, and these were later followed by many more taken on the moat bridge and in the gardens.

Jon and Fiona's wedding day

A large marquee in the extensive grounds accommodated the 100 family members, friends and colleagues who had been invited to share Jon and Fiona's special day.

The house is rich in history and contains a room which has its own unique story. In the early eighteenth century George Sacheverell, whose family owned the house, was imprisoned within that room's four walls for many years. He had committed no greater crime than simply to fall in love with a French maid, but this had clearly incurred the wrath of his prominent family. The room had only small windows which provided little light, but in spite of this the lovesick aristocrat passed his many solitary hours etching poignant love poems in French upon the walls of the dingy room.

Leaving aside this unhappy episode in the castle's history, Fiona and Jon enjoyed a wonderful and glorious day which they and their guests will always remember.

I imagine that Lisa, who is always so caring towards each and every member of our family, must at some time during the day have reflected upon her own marriage to Brian in 1980, when their wedding reception was held at another historic building – the famous Stone Manor, near Kidderminster. It was a most happy day, despite the fact that the heavens opened and rain poured down as she and I were driven in a vintage car to the ceremony at Old Swinford church, a building she loved to visit because of its history and wonderful atmosphere. Later, the dismal weather took a turn for the better, and after the ceremony the sun shone brightly and lent a special bonus to the day.

Regrettably, in 1996 Lisa and Brian separated and Lisa was granted custody of their two sons, Tristan and Jamie, who were then aged fourteen and twelve.

To her great credit she has brought them up exceedingly well and ensured that they were educated to a high standard at Old Swinford School, a well-respected Midlands educational establishment. Lisa's upbringing of my grandsons, and her attention to their education, ensured that they were each able to go on to university. At times it must have placed a considerable strain on her, but they are a great credit to her and a source of enormous pride to me.

* * * *

As one grows older, moments of particular happiness inevitably tend to drift more frequently across the field of memory. In my own case, so many of these memories pertain to Lisa and Jonathan that I would have to write a completely separate book to encompass them all. Of course, some of them are so personal and precious that to write about them would be to take away a little of the beauty which age treasures.

Because our children are born of us, each and every parent can be forgiven for thinking their own children are unique. Without wishing, therefore, to go beyond the bounds of reality, I can say without hesitation that my own children's loving care and unlimited kindness, particularly when I have most needed it during times of illness or sadness, have been a true blessing. Neither of them would wish for any praise in this regard, but, lest I should ever forget, I want to make special mention of it here.

There is a well-known saying that grandchildren can be a source of great joy when they are with you, but what a relief it is when they go back home to their parents! I am not sure I would always agree with that statement, for when over the years Heather and I had charge of our brood – Tristan, Jamie, Alexandra, Philippa and Ella – they have almost invariably brought us great joy and delight. Of course, their youthful enthusiasm and boundless energy, along with the occasional bout of bickering, have sometimes left us tired, but those contrasts have in themselves taught us that real happiness has two sides, and it is only the testing of those extremes which can bring that rarest of gifts – true and unconditional love.

I now observe the continuing unfoldment of their personalities, and look on with pride as the eldest four take up the challenges of adult life.

Tristan, now twenty-eight, took a gap year from his studies before becoming a student at the University of the West of England. In that year, he travelled to Whistler, in Canada, doing a variety of jobs, many of them manual, but this was no hardship to him for he had already worked with a local builder doing all kinds of tasks. Returning to take up his place at university, he graduated as a sports therapist, with a special emphasis on injury repairs.

Graduation days for Tristan and Alexandra

What a change of occupation it was for him, then, when he joined Citigroup bankers at Canary Wharf. Since then he has been promoted several times and now holds a very responsible position.

His brother Jamie, now twenty-six years old, took time out after leaving school and worked at a number of jobs, one of them as a bartender at the Merry Hill Complex. He is currently working for a national company as an apprentice quantity surveyor and attends Wolverhampton University on day release to further his studies. He hopes to graduate shortly.

Aside from his studies, Jamie has become an expert kickboxer, and competed with his team members in the 2009 European championships.

Alex is twenty-three, graduated from Birmingham University in 2009 and is now a qualified teacher. She was soon appointed to a school in Wolverhampton and has recently moved on to teach at a larger school in West Bromwich. She is also a qualified teacher of dancing.

Philippa will celebrate her twenty-first birthday in December 2010 and is in her final year at Birmingham University. She is studying a course on Media, Culture and

Society but has not yet decided which career path she will follow. She is also a qualified dance teacher. Like her sister, Alex, she is a kind-hearted person and has recently spent some time in Ghana, helping disadvantaged young people.

Both Alex and Philippa are very caring towards their mother, Jane, who is quite seriously incapacitated following a botched spinal operation. Despite what she has to bear, Jane – a talented violinist – is exceedingly brave and determined.

My youngest granddaughter, Ella, is now eight years old and lives with her mother just outside Chesterfield. Jonathan collects her every second weekend and often brings her to see me when she is with him and Fiona for the weekend. She is bright and well behaved, and loves her school.

If I have any regret at all about my family, it is only that I don't see enough of my two great-grandsons, Max and Joshua. They are lovely little boys, but, sadly for me, live some distance away in Chelmsford.

* * * *

I have already mentioned that my sister Laura, four years older than I, played a significant role in prompting my early enquiries into Spiritualism. It would be remiss of me, though, if I did not make mention of the enormous help, advice and encouragement I received from her subsequently, stretching back to the earliest days of my involvement with Stourbridge church.

There were times when she would reprimand me for my approach to certain issues, and she was frequently correct. On one such occasion I told her of my frustrations after being out-voted at a committee meeting. I had wanted the church to buy the house next door, together with all its land, for I hoped to turn the house into a residential home for all Spiritualists, and the land would have been invaluable as an additional parking area for the church. However, I was not successful in getting the committee to agree about purchasing the greater section of land I had persuaded the owner to split off.

Laura was having none of my frustrations. 'For goodness sake!' she said to me. 'You can't always be right. Grow up!' I took the knuckle rap in good part, and the piece of land we did eventually purchase turned out to be invaluable and has since enabled us to accommodate all the many cars which bring people to our services week by week.

On another occasion, I arrived to visit Laura and Ray following a SNU council meeting at Stansted Hall. Laura took one look at me and said with concern, 'You look tired and pale, Eric. What's the matter?'

I reluctantly explained that I had taken some flak from members of the council, and from a member of the NEC who should have supported me. I had been put in the hot seat at the very last minute, since Gordon Higginson had a speaking engagement in some far-flung part of the country, and as vice-president I had had to chair the meeting in his place.

Throughout her life, Laura's nature was never one of envy or offensiveness. She would always look on the bright side and think the best of people, sometimes saying, 'I don't really like them for their behaviour, but I love them all the same.'

And so she responded, 'I don't know why you're complaining, Eric. It just shows what trust Gordon has in you. Be glad that you had the honour.' Honour? She was right again.

Whilst Laura never played a part in committee, or in any other area of the church's administration, she was by virtue of her kind and generous nature a pillar of the place, and greatly loved by all. She and her husband Ray shared fifty years of happy life together, even though some of them were testing and hard-going when money was tight and they were raising their two daughters, Julie and Linda. Although I tried in my own way, as did Heather, nothing could ever have recompensed her sufficiently for what she did for me. She was an angel.

As Laura and Ray grew older, they lived in a flat, happy and contented, until they each had a series of falls. In a desire to ensure their safety, the local authority found them a place in a local residential home, but after several weeks their daughter Linda, who lives in Gloucestershire, made arrangements with Dudley and Gloucester authorities to have them transferred to a residential home in Tetbury. It was an excellent place, quite literally next door to Linda's own home. It was a wonderful solution, since it enabled Linda and her family to visit Laura and Ray on a daily basis.

Visiting them myself, I was able to observe the caring staff, the excellent food, and other amenities of a very high order, which were exceptional and much appreciated by Laura, Ray, and all of us who love them.

Throughout her life Laura had a remarkable memory and could recall in fine detail events which had occurred seventy or more years ago. She was especially fond of recounting those which related to my wayward life as a youngster, which sometimes left me red-faced, but caused great delight to Heather, our children and grandchildren!

Relaxing in Cambridge with Laura, Ray and friends

Chapter 17

Stopped in my tracks

During the month of February 2009, I was rushed to hospital in excruciating pain. After hurried tests I was told that I had a stark choice to make. Either I had an emergency operation or I would be dead within three hours.

The operation was a serious one, involving the removal of one metre of my intestine, and was carried out by a very skilful lady surgeon. It transpired that an operation to remove my appendix, some seventy-four years earlier, had left scar tissue which was pressing down on my intestine and had caused the current problem.

Though the operation itself was successful, the days and weeks which followed brought many other health problems. It was as if the shock to my system had rendered me open to all manner of ailments and emergencies. As I lay in my hospital bed one day, my blood pressure plummeted, and within minutes nine doctors were packed into my room, struggling to save me. Despite the frantic activity raging all around me, I seemed to remain curiously calm as I watched the efforts of the staff. They were agitated, trying unsuccessfully to get a line into me and making a pig's ear of it. One of them said to another, 'Get out of the bloody way!' He was the one who eventually managed it.

Following a month in hospital as I recovered from such major surgery, I was transferred to a convalescent home in Netherton, on the outskirts of Dudley, so that I could continue the slow and rather tedious process of regaining my strength before returning home. To say the least, it was not the happiest of times for me. I had lost a great deal of weight, and when I suffered occasional attacks of dizziness and nausea as a result of the Meniere's disease with which I had been diagnosed years earlier, I felt drained and weak as a kitten.

Most of the people in the home were as old, if not older than I was, and acted while there as though they had lost all incentive to live. Many had to be led to the table at meal times, and afterwards were either taken straight back to their respective rooms or placed in chairs in front of the television. It was a way of life I found utterly demoralising, and it made me all the more determined to get well enough to leave.

Throughout this time I was kept up to date with news of our church by my very capable vice-president Laraine Killarney, who visited me frequently. No amount of thanks would be adequate for the excellent way she ensured the smooth running of such a busy church during my enforced absence. In this she was supported by our honorary vice-president, Ron Pratt, and other members of our church community.

In May I was pronounced fit enough to return home, though with a lot of support from district nursing staff and other carers who visited me on a daily basis. Though I appreciated and certainly needed this care, there was no denying that my lack of independence frustrated me greatly and I longed to be properly self-sufficient again. Ten days after returning to the comfort and peace of my own home I found myself back in hospital – the result of a minor stroke.

Lying yet again in a hospital bed, I felt a little low, and was depressingly aware of how dreary life had become for me, particularly since I still have quite an active brain and have always been busy in one way or another. Time dragged, and my thoughts inevitably turned to the events of earlier times.

I have already written about my years as a flight sergeant in the Air Training Corps during the 1940s, and as my mind drifted I recalled a fellow named Bill Longmore, who had

been a colleague at that time. He was a very tall chap –
perhaps six-feet two or three – and had bright red hair. By
nature he was a quiet, gentle soul, a lovely young man.

Bill eventually left the corps to join the Royal Air Force
and, following training, took his place as a crew member on
a bomber plane. On his very first flight the plane was shot
down over Germany and he was killed.

His mother and father, who, like their son, were very
gentle people, lived in a small council house in Brierley Hill.
They let me know about Bill's passing, and I went along to
see them. It was a visit I have never quite been able to forget,
for I feel that in some way I failed those people, who were in
such pain.

As I sat and talked with Bill's parents, his mother raised
her eyes to me and asked the only question that had any
meaning for her. 'Eric,' she said pleadingly, 'Can you tell me
where my boy has gone?'

Even as I write this now there are goose pimples on my
arms. There was heart-rending sadness in her voice. Her son
had been a lovely boy and should not have been killed at such
a young age. I was out of my depth. I had not long been
interested in Spiritualism and had no experience of dealing
with such vexed situations. Perhaps I was too unsure of my
ground; perhaps I feared that Bill's mother and father were
so devastated by their loss that it would be unwise for me to
tell them what I knew about the continuity of life. Either way,
I could offer them no real answer.

After a while the Longmores moved out of the area and I
lost touch with them, but I often wondered how they would
manage to come to terms with their terrible and sudden loss
until such time as they could meet their beloved Bill again.

In the years that have followed I have always kicked
myself that I was not able to think of something to say that
might have helped to ease their pain.

* * * *

As July approached and I continued to recover quietly at home, the SNU's annual general meeting drew near. I knew I would not be well enough to attend it, and thus missed the event for only the second time in sixty years. I later learned that, in my absence, it had been announced that I was to receive a unique award. Friends told me that following the announcement delegates rose unanimously to their feet and gave a lengthy standing ovation. I was deeply touched by that.

It was soon arranged that the award would be presented to me during a special service at Stourbridge church on 9th August. Although I had a vague idea of what to expect, I played no part in the arrangements, for my fragile state of health meant that responsibility for the day-to-day running of the church was still in the hands of Laraine, who did her utmost to spare me from any stress and strain, and kept the finer details of the event a closely guarded secret.

Perhaps it was simply because I was still not feeling too well, but for whatever reason, the significance of the award just hadn't hit home to me. Consequently, as I walked into the church with my family, I was utterly and absolutely overwhelmed to see so many people there. The place was packed, with an overflow of people standing in the hallway, and I was greatly moved by the generous greetings offered to me as I made my way up the church on the arm of my eldest granddaughter, Alexandra.

The editor of *Psychic News* travelled to Stourbridge to attend the presentation, and a few days later her account of it appeared in the paper.

This is what she wrote:

Spiritualism's much-loved ambassador has been presented with a newly created award in recognition of his lifetime of outstanding service to the Spiritualist movement.

On Sunday 9th August, Laraine Killarney, Vice-President of Stourbridge National Spiritualist Church, welcomed more than two hundred people who had gathered at a Divine Service to honour Minister Eric

Hatton, President of the church for several decades, and Honorary President of the Spiritualists' National Union.

After introducing Janet Parker, the medium and speaker for the service, Mrs Killarney invited the congregation to unite in sending out thoughts of healing to all who were in need, following which the healing hymn was played by the organist, Geoff Heath.

Janet Parker then gave the address, in which she spoke warmly of Eric Hatton's unique contribution to Spiritualism, after which a hymn was sung, and was followed by a demonstration of spirit communication.

Laraine Killarney then invited Minister Duncan Gascoyne, President of the Spiritualists' National Union, to come to the platform.

Addressing the congregation, Mr Gascoyne said: 'Tonight is extra special because we are here to pay tribute to a gentleman – Minister Eric Hatton. We are celebrating a life of service.'

Recalling former SNU President Ernest Oaten, the first person ever to make a BBC broadcast about Spiritualism, Mr Gascoyne said: 'Eric and Ernest Oaten are out of the same mould. Ernest put his heart and soul into the movement and Eric has done the same.'

Referring to other awards made by the Union, such as certificates and diplomas, he said: 'A piece of paper would not be good enough for you, Eric, so we've done something different, because you are a unique person.' He then presented to Mr Hatton the Lifetime Achievement Award for Services to Spiritualism, a distinctive engraved plaque of glass over metal.

Responding to Mr Gascoyne's earlier summary of the manifold ways in which he had served the cause of Spiritualism – as SNU president and vice-president, chairman of numerous bodies and in a multitude of other capacities – Mr Hatton, who has been a Spiritualist for 66 years, said, 'I am overwhelmed that I have been honoured in such a way.'

He then paid tribute to the enormous support given to him by Heather, his wife of more than 50 years, who passed to spirit in June 2007.

'Had it not been that Heather was as dedicated, perhaps more dedicated, than me, I do not know how I would have been able to achieve the things I've done.'

Offering his sincere thanks to those present, who had travelled from all parts of the country to attend the service, and expressing particular gratitude for the great happiness he had derived from the support of his family, many of whom were present, Mr Hatton spoke of his hopes for the future of Spiritualism.

'Ours is a practical religion – a far-seeing religion. I only hope that when I move on – and I will move on – not only this church, but the movement we have been proud to serve, will continue to serve in strength and in loyalty, and also to give great solace to people who are bereaved.'

Speaking with much emotion, he concluded, "May I thank you all for giving me the honour of being here, for this award and for all the things that you have given me which have enriched my life."

A heartfelt and lengthy standing ovation followed Mr Hatton's words.

Officers of the SNU had travelled to Stourbridge to take part in the historic presentation, and made their way to the platform to pay tribute to Mr Hatton. First to speak was the Union's Vice-President (Administrative), Minister Dinah Annable. Turning to Mr Hatton, she said:

'Eric, may I say how honoured I am to be here today? I would not have missed this for the world.' Recalling the day she had first been due to meet Mr Hatton, she told the congregation that she had been nervous and a little in awe. 'But the moment we met and spoke, you put me at my ease.

And I have found over all these subsequent years that you have a magic way of putting people at their ease.'

Vice-President (Spiritual) Minister Judith Seaman spoke next, recalling the time when Eric Hatton had been president of the Union, and Tim Horton the treasurer. 'I was like a child in a sweetshop,' she said, 'sitting and listening to these two elder statesmen of Spiritualism tell their stories of the pioneers they'd known, the people they'd sat with and the mediumship they'd witnessed. And wow, was that a privilege to me.'

She then explained that the officers of the Union wanted to make a personal presentation. 'Ours is a religion of continuous life,' she said, 'so as a personal gift to you we have chosen a rose tree which will blossom for ever and ever. It will also symbolise how you have blossomed in all our lives and made such an impression upon us. For that, we thank you.'

Standing to accept the gift, Mr Hatton revealed that just three days earlier he had said to his daughter that he would like to buy a rose bush to dedicate to his wife, Heather. His daughter had told him, 'Don't do that. Wait until you feel you have touched the right one.'

Duncan Gascoyne then added that a pink rose had been chosen expressly to symbolise the love and affection people felt for Mr Hatton.

Financial Director David Bruton then took the microphone, saying: 'Luckily for me, I was introduced to Eric when I was just eighteen. Over the last 30 years I have come to consider him a very dear friend – a gentleman for whom I will always have a great deal of respect. For what he does, for what he gives, for his touch which is so very special.'

Addressing Eric Hatton directly, he continued: 'I am privileged to be part of tonight's proceedings, to honour in a small way your mighty contribution to this wonderful movement of Spiritualism – a movement we all love so dearly.'

The SNU's General Secretary Charles Coulston then spoke, describing Mr Hatton as 'a wise man' and 'a past master of self-effacement.'

'People, they say, are equal in Spiritualism under our wonderful principle of the Brotherhood of Man,' he continued. 'But we all recognise in our lives those who have in some measure imbibed the true meaning of Spiritualism and lived it in their lives, and they act as a beacon to all of us.

'In the years that Eric was president, that is how I saw him. He was the kind of man you wanted to emulate. You wanted to draw within your own attitude and stance towards the world the qualities and characteristics that Eric brought to the job.

'He was quiet and calm – could always see both sides of the question.

He always impressed me with his affability; he radiated a spiritual presence which made you want to be with him.'

Following these tributes, spoken with deep sincerity, Laraine Killarney invited the congregation to join in a final hymn, after which Janet Parker offered a closing prayer.

This unique evening was organised with loving care by Laraine Killarney and her fellow committee members. She told Psychic News: 'If everybody could be just half the person of Eric and Heather, there would be no wars, no poverty in this world. Eric has been my mentor – an inspiration and an example of what a person should be.'

It has delighted many that, in selecting a title for this award, the SNU has chosen to use the words 'Services to Spiritualism' rather than 'Services to the SNU', an inclusive and fitting recognition of the unique esteem in which Mr Hatton is held throughout the entire Spiritualist movement.

It is difficult to convey in words the extraordinary outpouring of affection directed towards Eric Hatton during this very special occasion. All present felt privileged to have witnessed the honouring of a true pioneer of Spiritualism.

The presentation of my award for 'Services to Spiritualism'

Of course, I will never know exactly why such a unique award was made to me. I can only assume that it was on the basis of my many years of involvement in Spiritualism. Very rarely had I been in any confrontation with anyone about the running of the movement, though I had certainly expressed my views and opinions when necessary. It may also have been due to the fact that I had been instrumental in achieving a number of things for the benefit of the Arthur Findlay College, and for the movement as a whole. Or perhaps it had something to do with my devotion over so many years to Stourbridge church, which has rarely had any problems because I have always tried to ensure that its running was conducted in a right and proper way. It would certainly seem that I had earned great respect from Spiritualists all over the country, for, as the *Psychic News* article pointed out, many of them had travelled long distances to be present at the service. Whatever the reasons for the award, it was an honour to receive it, and a memory I shall always treasure.

* * * *

Two months after that special service I embarked on the process of writing this book, and slowly regaining my strength began once again to take an active part in the running of Stourbridge church. Over the past year, though subject to various physical ups and downs, I have been well enough to conduct funerals, weddings and naming ceremonies, and even to sing again at some of our church events. I have also taken part in several church rededication ceremonies. In many ways it has been a remarkable recovery, causing a degree of amazement to my doctors, who show some slight interest when I explain that I have received much spiritual healing in addition to their own excellent care.

Although throughout my life I have read widely on many alternative and complementary treatment methods, and in some cases studied or been involved in their techniques, in recent times I have relied more heavily on the NHS to treat and heal some of my problems. It would therefore be remiss of me if I did not pay tribute in these pages to the many nurses, doctors and other practitioners who have shown me such great kindness as well as excellent professional care.

As I have already mentioned, on several occasions I have been admitted to, or attended outpatient clinics at Russells Hall Hospital, approximately six miles from my home. Over the last nine years it has been considerably enlarged and has greatly expanded the range of treatments and services it offers. Inevitably there have been complaints from some patients and their families but many of these have resulted from impatience or a lack of understanding of what is possible.

The immensity of the whole operation of a hospital that size is bound occasionally to fall short of the ideal standards its staff might wish to reach. If it were not for the great irritation of parking problems, the grouses of patients and visitors would perhaps be far fewer!

And so, if the thanks and reflections of one grateful patient have meaning to the staff, I hope they will take heart and be assured that I am not alone. From much personal experience, I say: 'Russells Hall, the home of excellence.'

* * * *

The same annual general meeting delegates who had so generously applauded the decision to give me a Lifetime Achievement Award had also voted almost unanimously for the building of a national memorial to Spiritualists who had lost their lives in the service of their country. It was to be erected in the country setting of Staffordshire's National Memorial Arboretum.

It had been made clear in *Psychic News* that this memorial was to be erected for all Spiritualists, not just those of the SNU. When I made enquiries of the then president, Duncan Gascoyne, during the early months of the fund-raising appeal, I was led to understand that letters had gone out to other Spiritualist organisations in the UK, yet their response had at best been indifferent, and in one or two cases actually negative.

It saddened me, both in the lead up to the installation of the memorial, and at the dedication service itself, that those who were involved in raising the necessary money, and those who attended the event, were almost exclusively from the SNU community. As a result, a significant opportunity was missed whereby the memorial could have served as a united Spiritualist tribute to those who have died. Whatever the differences between the various Spiritualist organisations, our common theme is surely that we believe in, and try to prove the reality of, life after death and the philosophical implications that go with it. Yet we fail to agree amongst ourselves as to what should constitute a unity of thought and ideas.

On 3rd July 2010, just days before the dedication of the new memorial in which I had been invited to play a part, I received the sad news that my wonderful, caring and talented sister Laura had passed from this life into the realm where our parents, brother Bert and Laura's own daughter, Julie, were waiting to welcome her. Since then, she has made her presence known through three different mediums, assuring me, her husband Ray and

Laura Fisher

daughter Linda of the joy she has found in her new life.

Of course, Laura's very recent passing added even greater poignancy to the service at the National Memorial Arboretum, at which the Last Post was played by a bugler from the Royal Marines and I was privileged to lay a commemorative wreath jointly with a young serving soldier named Philip Bradley.

Laying a wreath at the new National Memorial

As I said earlier in this book, our fragmented state has caused us to be seen as a somewhat 'disorganised rabble', with no cohesion on many points. Whilst I am proud of the fact that we now have such a memorial, I have to confess that I think it second best to our having formal representation at the Cenotaph on Remembrance Day. Until such time as we can attain that recognition for Spiritualism, I shall always feel that there is an 'arms-length' attitude toward us from government. Of course, it may well be that they are looking at the larger picture and see that after all these years we still haven't agreed to agree amongst ourselves. Our differences have kept us apart and prevented us from becoming a united movement.

* * * *

As my book was about to go to press, I received word of two events which have cast a cloud of sadness over its conclusion. Two valued friends I have worked with and admired for many years passed on within days of each other.

Professor David Fontana

The noted psychologist Professor David Fontana died on 18th October following a short illness. On each occasion we met he inspired me with his considerable knowledge on a wide range of subjects, particularly psychical matters, to which he devoted decades of research, becoming a leading authority. His knowledge of world religions and their practices was similarly impressive.

David was an active member of the renowned Society for Psychical Research and served as its president from 1995 to 1998. In all that he did, David displayed kindness and humility, together with the keenest intelligence, earning him respect and praise from many. In 2007 I invited him to Stansted Hall to give a series of talks during our annual Stourbridge week. His topics included psychical research outside Europe and the practicalities of developing spiritual awareness. During the course of that week, David and I discussed his cherished aim to see the full and unabridged story of Alec Harris's remarkable mediumship in print for the first time. With funding from the J.V. Trust, this dream became a reality in 2009.

David was in the process of writing a foreword to this book when he died. His passing came all too soon in my view, for there was still so much he could have offered to our world.

Just five days after David's passing, news reached me that Tom Harrison had also moved on to the next stage of life, at the venerable age of 92. Coincidentally, the two men had been great friends.

It is now about forty-five years since I first met Tom, for even though he had been involved in the Spiritualist scene for so many years before I was, our paths had never crossed. With his appointment as founder manager of the Arthur Findlay College, I had the privilege of sharing many moments with Tom, his wife Doris and their children. At that time,

Tom giving what was to be his last talk, at
Stansted Hall on J.V. Trust week in August 2010

financial matters troubled the college's board of management, and things were sometimes quite stressful, but we all made a point of relaxing when the work was done and almost always spent our leisure time in an atmosphere of joviality.

Tom had spiritual qualities which were inculcated within him by his Spiritualist upbringing, particularly by his having witnessed remarkable materialisation mediumship through his mother, Minnie, who was endowed with an outstanding gift. In the years that followed Minnie's passing in 1958, Tom made it his mission to talk, lecture and illustrate with slides the many wonderful events that had taken place in her séance room, bringing conviction of the reality of life after death to countless people. Tom's first wife Doris passed on in 1976 but he continued his work to spread the truth of survival. In 1998, he married Ann, who greatly assisted him in that work.

My later encounters with Tom were all too infrequent, but in August 2010 we were privileged to have him as an honoured guest at J.V. Trust week, during which he gave, with Ann's assistance, an extraordinary talk on the materialisation mediumship of his mother. My appreciation of him has only been strengthened with the passage of time, and our meetings over the past two years have reminded me yet again what a privilege has been mine in knowing him.

Tom Harrison and I at my home in 2009

Afterword

After almost sixty-six years of involvement and research in Spiritualism, I have concluded how little I know of its true purpose. I write in this vein even though I have been privileged to see so much of its phenomena, and to witness some of the most remarkable instances of hearts being repaired after they have been broken by the loss of a loved one from this physical life.

Without the benefits and blessings of good mediumship, people from many walks of life would never have been able to take up the challenge to continue living. Indeed, many recipients of messages from loved ones in spirit would never have realised that there were indeed new and life-enhancing experiences still to be tasted – experiences which would enrich and inspire their continuing earthly journey.

Whilst applauding – and I always will – the importance of such noble work of mediumship, as I grow older I ask myself the question – What was the most important aspect of the many avenues of spirit I have explored? Please do not misunderstand me, I can never deny or change the wondrous things I have experienced, for some were almost beyond my comprehension. Most of these experiences were made possible by the dedication and sacrifice of sensitives – mediums – call them what you will. They came from all walks of life – some poor, others affluent; some educated, others entirely unschooled. The gift of mediumship transcends such worldly criteria.

True and dedicated mediumship, as opposed to simple psychic ability, in which no spirit communication is involved, has often been a costly calling for its practitioners, both in terms of time and deterioration of physical health. If, therefore, after witnessing this quality of mediumship, you should feel inspired to follow such examples, be aware that the requirements and demands are high and, of course, cannot be learned from books or tuition, important though these may be. For the way of such sensitivity must come as a result of being the recipient of a gift.

In the present era, when education in all fields is deemed a high priority, there can be a factor which we are in danger of overlooking. For whilst it is desirable, some may say vital, to require our mediums to have qualifications and letters after their names, there have been and always will be excellent mediums who cannot or do not wish to gain such accreditation. It is easy to offer reasons for this, one of them being that very good mediumship is in such demand that courses of study are nigh on impossible for its exponents because of the time factor. I could name several such persons whose evidential quality is amongst the best and highest it is possible to witness.

My plea, therefore, would be that we who call ourselves Spiritualists should not become too hidebound and restrictive in our desire to legislate. How many times have I heard the cry, 'Oh, not more rules and regulations!' However, it must also be said that without a degree of organisation we would sometimes be at a great disadvantage, particularly where our hope for recognition by either government or society in general is concerned.

There are many sincere people who, having searched for a spiritual meaning to life, and in the process having discovered communication between this physical world and the limitless world of eternity, will set up centres which do not always bring credit to the true essence of Spiritualism.

Experience shows me that there are churches, centres and groups of people who are supposed to have been enlightened by the impact of spiritual knowledge – knowledge which should have changed their lives. Yet because of disagreement they are blinkered, sometimes to the point of causing a split, which damages not only themselves but, more importantly, their own small communities.

I am reminded of the once thriving Apostolic churches which existed principally in Wales, and which, as a result of internal disagreements and an unwillingness to allow for human failings, broke up and no longer seem to be in existence.

This therefore prompts me to remind those who carry the weight of office in such bodies to exercise understanding coupled with discipline. I would plead with leaders at both local and national levels, no less than I would with mediums, to cultivate that most vital ingredient – humility.

I have already indicated that after six decades of searching, and of witnessing so many remarkable events, I am still unsure of my true purpose in life. As you will have detected, many of the events described in this book have had a profound influence on the direction of my journey through life. For though it seems that experience needs to be varied – for otherwise we would learn little from its contrasts – I ponder why, at the age of 84 years, and having seen clearly the beauty and glory of the etheric world, there are still (so I am told) things for me to do.

I cannot change from being called a Spiritualist, for it is through this gateway that my eyes have been opened. The Seven Principles of Spiritualism offer guidance to each one of us, as they have certainly done for me, yet my soul cries out for that elusive something which is deeper than anything I can comprehend. Is it that in realising my relationship with all God's creation I have the hunger of the universal mystic, wanting things to be defined, yet sensing within me that there are many aspects of my 'destiny' which urge me to continue the journey? For I acknowledge, as do many other searchers, that life both here and in the next phases of the eternal world is but a part of the glorious reality. You must judge for yourselves where you stand in this particular moment of time, but I hope with all my heart that you will find fulfilment.

In writing this book I have tried to show, from my humble beginnings, a little of my sense of uncertainty in interpreting and expressing the ultimate purpose of the wonders I have experienced, but also at the same time to record my thanks to the Eternal Spirit, whom we call God, for granting me these priceless gifts of experience and revelation.

Could it be that in bearing witness to these wonders I have but touched the fringe of his ways?

How did man come to be?

Tell me, my friend, what has your life's experience taught?
Are you a man of dreams, or just a man of action?
Seek you to drown the truth with wine of mere distraction?
Or with the more corrosive opiate of thought?

Are you contented with dull prose of life's expression,
Or do you bear the poetry of Nature's voice?
There have been moments when you had to make your choice;
Chose you the ugly or the beautiful impression?

Some see in life a jungle of annihilation,
Others a counting-house for storing wealth within;
Some see a mask for columbine and harlequin,
And others a Gethsemane for meditation.

Tell me, my friend, to what illusions you have clung;
We can but hope to dream of light, whose eyes are bound;
In this dark forest of our hopes, what have you found –
Or am I speaking to you in a foreign tongue?

Cyril Upton
(Musings in Provence)

Author's Note

Those who know and have worked alongside Sue Farrow, the former editor of *Psychic News*, have long been aware of her considerable ability in the journalistic field. It is only by working with her, which has been my privilege over the past year, that I have fully recognised the extent of her talent in this demanding profession.

Without her collaboration as editor of my autobiography, as well as her guidance in the relaying of my life's chapters, the book would not have been possible, for while the details of my experiences have been mine alone, the moulding and compiling of them has been Sue's. Thanks to her cannot be enough for the times when she has been my mentor during the process of writing, particularly when hurdles arose and had to be negotiated.

In preparing the book, there were occasions when I wondered whether some of my experiences were so unusual as to give rise to scepticism and doubt in the mind of my readers, despite the fact that they represent a true and accurate record. At such times these doubts were always discussed with Sue and reasoned out by her.

If, therefore, you have found this book enjoyable as well as challenging, it is in large part due to Sue, for, though many others have asked me to share my experiences, without her my story would never have been told.

Lightning Source UK Ltd.
Milton Keynes UK

172123UK00007B/57/P